THE
CLASSICO™/MC®
PASTA SAUCE
COOKBOOK

THE
CLASSICO™/MC
®
PASTA SAUCE
COOKBOOK

Antigone Dallas

Robert
ROSE

The Classico Pasta Sauce Cookbook
Text copyright © 2002 Antigone Dallas
Photographs copyright © 2002 Robert Rose Inc.

For complete cataloguing information, see page 184.

Disclaimer
The recipes in this book have been carefully tested by our kitchen and our tasters. To the best of our knowledge, they are safe and nutritious for ordinary use and users. For those people with food or other allergies, or who have special food requirements or health issues, please read the suggested contents of each recipe carefully and determine whether or not they may create a problem for you. All recipes are used at the risk of the consumer.

We cannot be responsible for any hazards, loss or damage that may occur as a result of any recipe use.

For those with special needs, allergies, requirements or health problems, in the event of any doubt, please contact your medical adviser prior to the use of any recipe.

Design & Production: PageWave Graphics Inc.
Editor: Carol Sherman
Copy Editor: Deborah Aldcorn
Assistant Recipe Developer: Donna Bartolini

Original photography including cover: Robert Wigington; pages 10, 15, 26, 31, 35, 39, 65, 69, 78, 83, 95, 105, 112, 119, 123, 127, 131, 132, 141, 145, 149, 150, 155, 161, 165, 166, 175, 179, 183
    Food Stylist: Ruth Gangbar
    Props Stylist: Susan Florian

Additional photography:
Doug Bradshaw; pages 19, 47, 51, 91, 108, 159
Peter Chou; pages 23, 99
Yvonne Duivenvoorden; pages 59, 117, 137, 171
Steve Elphick; pages 42, 73
Robert Wigington; pages 55, 63, 77

Color Scans: Colour Technologies

Cover image: Chicken and Asparagus Toss (see recipe variation, page 112)
Photo page 2: Penne with Leek, Smoked Ham and Asparagus (see recipe, page 58)
Photo page 6: Chickpea Salad with Grilled Shrimp (see recipe, page 38)

We acknowledge the financial support of the Government of Canada through the Book Publishing Industry Development Program (BPIDP) for our publishing activities.

Published by: Robert Rose Inc.
120 Eglinton Ave. E., Suite 1000, Toronto, Ontario, Canada M4P 1E2
Tel: (416) 322-6552   Fax: (416) 322-6936

Printed in Canada
1 2 3 4 5 6 7 8 9 10   FC   09 08 07 06 05 04 03 02

Contents

Introduction

At Classico, we are very proud of the Old World craftsmanship that goes into our specially prepared sauces. We use only the finest ingredients, such as vine-ripened tomatoes, pure olive oil and aromatic cheeses, and select the best herbs and spices to complement their rich flavors. These genuine Italian ingredients are carefully combined to create the delicious homemade taste you have come to expect from Classico.

Our commitment to quality allows you to enjoy the best authentically Italian sauces in the comfort of your home, with none of the effort they traditionally demand. We bring the flavors, colors and textures of Italy to North American kitchens in a variety of sauces that are delicious, not only over pasta but also as a major component of many other dishes including appetizers, pizzas, stews and casseroles. At Classico, we do the work so you can enjoy the compliments.

Now, with the publication of *The Classico Pasta Sauce Cookbook*, we have taken our commitment to quality and convenience one step further. Containing more than 100 easy-to-follow recipes for a dazzling collection of dishes that will meet your every need, from snacks and casual family meals to the most elegant dinner parties, this book will get you from the recipe to the table as quickly and easily as possible. And with superlative results!

Since pasta is the first image that usually comes to mind whenever Italian food is mentioned, it almost goes without saying that great pasta recipes will be a highlight of any book featuring Classico sauces. Delicious, nutritious and infinitely varied, pasta has become the ideal mealtime solution for busy weeknights in North America. With *The Classico Pasta Sauce Cookbook*, you can select from great family-style recipes, such as *Cheese-Filled Tortellini with Fresh Basil* or *Asparagus and Mushrooms Noodles Alfredo*, to satisfying dinners that taste as if you've been slaving in the kitchen for hours. Although equally effortless, more sophisticated recipes, such as *Creamy Seafood Fettuccine* or *Penne with Leek, Smoked Ham and Asparagus*, are elegant enough to serve to guests. Even better, having a collection of superb pasta recipes on hand allows you to leverage the versatility of this popular food. Reduce the serving size and offer pasta for a first course, as it's done in Italy, or add salad and crusty Italian bread to serve a great North American-style meal.

But pasta is only one of the great glories of Italian food. In these pages, you will also find an abundance of inspirational ideas illustrating how Classico sauces can be used as the foundation for many other delectable combinations, from *Tuscan Chicken with Garlic and Capers* to *Mediterranean Fish Stew*. Using these recipes, you will be able to create rich, colorful and delicious dishes for almost every course. All the recipes have been developed with today's busy families in mind. They are simple to make, yet filled with flavor. With a minimum of effort you'll soon be transforming everyday meals into eagerly anticipated events, full of new and exciting tastes.

Choose from a selection of delicious appetizers to get dinner off to a great start. In these pages, you'll find tasty starters, such as *Eggplant and Cheese Rolls*, *Garlic Shrimp* or *Sun-Dried Tomato, Mushroom and Goat Cheese Toasts*. All will whet your taste buds and sharpen your appetite for pleasures to come. Some, such as *Grilled Polenta with Roasted Portobello Mushroom*, *White Bean Dip with Lemon* or *Sun-Dried Tomato Artichoke Dip*, can even do double duty as a light meal or snack.

And don't forget the salad course. Today, salads are much more than assorted greens, tossed with oil and vinegar. While delicious combinations such as *Tomato and Bocconcini Cheese Salad* are the perfect finish to any meal, we've also included recipes for more substantial salads, which can be used in a variety of ways. Try using *Three-Bean and Corn Salad* to add color to a buffet table or serve guests our unique *Potato Salad*, enhanced with sun-dried tomato pesto, to add zest to a summer barbecue. Be sure to accompany these salads with lots of crusty Italian bread, as diners will want to soak up and savor their luscious dressings.

We've also included a cornucopia of soups, stews and casseroles to satisfy your longing for heartier foods. Chock-full of flavorful and nutritious ingredients, soups such as *Sweet Corn, Sausage and Tomato Soup* and *Potato and Garlic Soup*, are hearty enough to be the focus of a light supper. More substantial dishes, such as *Home-Style Beef Stew* and *Sausage, Pepper and Tomato Toss*, make rich and satisfying meals. And versatile casseroles, such as *Cabbage Rolls*, *Lasagna Florentine* and *Layered Eggplant Casserole*, are as appropriate on a party buffet table as they are at potlucks or family dinners.

If you have vegetarians in your circle, you'll welcome the resource of recipes that meet their dietary needs. Dishes such as *Leek, Gruyère and Sun-Dried Tomato Pesto Tart* and *Roasted Vegetable Frittata with Goat Cheese* are so packed with flavor that even non-vegetarians will want seconds.

Of course, no cookbook would be complete without ideas for bringing out the best in the traditional main course staples: meat, poultry and fish. With an abundance of mouth-watering meat dishes that include *Rice and Beef-Stuffed Peppers*, *Roast Leg of Lamb with Tomato, Artichoke and Peppers* and *Sun-Dried Tomato Pesto and Cheese-Stuffed Pork Chops*, *The Classico Pasta Sauce Cookbook* will help to perk up even the most jaded palates. And if, like many people, you can't get through the week without at least one meal featuring chicken, you'll welcome the collection of innovative poultry recipes, including *Braised Chicken with Eggplant*, *Chicken Sauté with Sun-Dried Tomatoes* and *Four-Mushroom Chicken*. Fish dishes are equally original and run the gamut from *Halibut with Fennel and Tomato*, a simple bake with a roasted tomato and garlic sauce, to more elaborate presentations such as *Crab-Stuffed Sole*.

Whether your taste leans to cozy and informal or stylish and elegant, our collection of trouble-free recipes for entertaining will produce stunning results with a minimum of work. Set the table with your best tableware and linens and impress your guests with show-stopping main courses such as *Pesto-Crusted Rack of Lamb with Feta* and *Seared Halibut with Mussels and Clams*. For a casual evening with friends, toss a salad, open an bottle of Chianti and serve *Zucchini, Smoked Ham and Sun-Dried Tomato Risotto*. No one will know that you didn't spend the day in the kitchen and you can relax and enjoy your company, knowing they will be savoring a delicious meal.

With a supply of Classico sauces in the pantry, you can produce flavorful and satisfying food that tastes homemade with a minimum of work. We hope this book will become an indispensable kitchen tool, helping you to prepare delicious meals with made-from-scratch taste every day of the week.

Appetizers

~

Eggplant with Goat Cheese
and Fire-Roasted Tomato *12*

Spinach, Feta and Sun-Dried Tomato Triangles *14*

Sun-Dried Tomato, Mushroom
and Goat Cheese Toasts *16*

Eggplant and Cheese Rolls *17*

Garlic Shrimp *18*

White Bean Dip with Lemon *20*

Sun-Dried Tomato Artichoke Dip *21*

Grilled Polenta with Roasted Portobello Mushroom *22*

Tomato Chili Hummus *24*

Brie and Onion Bake *25*

Eggplant with Goat Cheese and Fire-Roasted Tomato

Eggplant with Goat Cheese and Fire-Roasted Tomato

Here's a delicious starter that looks as good as it tastes. The superb combination of eggplant, goat cheese, sweet pepper and roasted tomatoes is mouth-watering.

SERVES 4

- PREHEAT OVEN TO 350°F (180°C)
- 8-CUP (2 L) BAKING DISH

	Salt	
1	large eggplant, sliced into 8 rounds, about ½-inch (1 cm) thick	1
	All-purpose flour	
1 cup	olive oil (approx.)	250 mL
4 oz	goat cheese	125 g
2 tbsp	finely diced roasted yellow bell pepper (see Tip, page 44)	25 mL
2 tbsp	finely chopped fresh parsley	25 mL
1	jar (26 oz/700 mL) Classico di Siena Fire-Roasted Tomato & Garlic Pasta Sauce	1
	Additional chopped fresh parsley, optional	

1. Lightly salt eggplant rounds and let stand for 30 minutes. Pat dry and then lightly toss in flour. Remove and set aside.

2. In a saucepan, heat 6 tbsp (90 mL) oil over medium-high heat and fry 3 to 4 eggplant rounds at a time, cooking until both sides are golden, adding more oil when required. Place cooked eggplant on paper towel-lined trays to absorb excess oil.

3. In a small bowl, combine goat cheese, roasted pepper and parsley.

4. Spread pasta sauce on baking dish. Place 4 eggplant slices on sauce and evenly cover each with the goat cheese mixture. Top with remaining eggplant slices.

5. Bake, uncovered, in preheated oven for 25 to 30 minutes. Serve eggplant rounds with sauce and top with a sprinkle of chopped parsley, if desired.

....

Tip: Grilling the sliced eggplant would work equally well in this recipe. Toss or brush the eggplant with olive oil until lightly coated. Place on a greased grill over medium heat. Cook, turning occasionally, until tender, about 8 to 10 minutes.

Other Great Recipes Featuring
Classico di Siena Fire-Roasted Tomato & Garlic Pasta Sauce

Fish and Seafood
Halibut with Fennel and Tomato (*page 138*)
Shrimp Jambalaya (*page 147*)

Lamb
Siena Lamb Chops (*page 104*)

Vegetarian
Vegetarian Chili (*page 156*)

For a complete list of recipes using this sauce,
see Index by Sauce (*page 185*).

Spinach, Feta and Sun-Dried Tomato Triangles

These savory appetizers put a contemporary spin on the classic feta and spinach pie. They will disappear quickly, so you may want to double, triple or even quadruple this recipe, depending on your guest list.

MAKES 16 HORS D'OEUVRES

- **PREHEAT OVEN TO 375°F (190°C)**
- **BAKING SHEETS, LINED WITH PARCHMENT PAPER**

½ cup	crumbled feta cheese	125 mL
½ cup	chopped, cooked spinach	125 mL
⅓ cup	Classico di Sardegna Sun-Dried Tomato Pesto	75 mL
1 tbsp	finely chopped fresh dill	15 mL
5	sheets phyllo pastry	5
¼ cup	butter, melted	50 mL

1. In a medium bowl, combine feta, spinach, pesto and dill.

2. Place one sheet of phyllo on work surface. Cover remaining sheets with plastic wrap and a damp cloth to prevent drying out. Brush sheet lightly with butter. Using a sharp knife cut lengthwise into four strips, each about 3 inches (7.5 cm) wide.

3. Spoon heaping tablespoonful (15 mL) spinach-pesto mixture about ½ inch (1 cm) from the bottom of one strip. Fold right corner across the filling to meet the left side to form a triangle. Continue folding pastry around the filling, maintaining a triangular shape. Do not wrap the triangle too tightly as filling will expand as it cooks. Continue folding triangle over and upward until end of strip is reached. Repeat with remaining strips of phyllo and remaining phyllo sheets and filling.

4. Place triangles on prepared baking sheets. Brush tops with butter. Bake in preheated oven until golden brown, about 15 to 18 minutes. Serve hot or at room temperature.

Tip: Freeze unbaked triangles on baking sheets, then store in a container for up to 6 weeks. Bake, frozen, until golden, about 18 to 22 minutes.

Variation

For bigger triangles suitable for a light lunch, use 4 sheets of phyllo dough. Brush one with butter, top with second sheet and brush with butter. Cut lengthwise in thirds. Using ¼ cup (50 mL) filling per strip of phyllo, roll up as indicated in recipe. Repeat with remaining phyllo and filling. Bake for 20 to 22 minutes. Serves 3.

Sun-Dried Tomato, Mushroom and Goat Cheese Toasts

These robust appetizers with velvety goat cheese are wonderfully easy and perfect for almost any occasion.

MAKES 24 HORS
D'OEUVRES

Variation
Substitute the goat cheese with feta or ricotta cheese.

• PREHEAT BROILER

2 tbsp	olive oil	25 mL
2 to 3	cloves garlic, minced	2 to 3
6 cups	sliced mushrooms, about 1 lb (500 g) (see Tip, below)	1.5 L
¼ tsp	salt	1 mL
¼ tsp	freshly ground black pepper	1 mL
1	baguette	1
½ cup	Classico di Sardegna Sun-Dried Tomato Pesto	125 mL
2 oz	goat cheese, crumbled	60 g

1. In a large skillet, heat oil over medium-high heat. Cook garlic, mushrooms, salt and pepper until liquid is evaporated and mushrooms are tender and brown, about 5 minutes.

2. Meanwhile, cut baguette into 24 slices. Broil until golden, about 30 seconds per side. Spread 1 tsp (5 mL) pesto on each baguette slice. Top with mushroom mixture. Sprinkle with goat cheese. Broil until cheese is melted, about 45 seconds.

Tip: To clean mushrooms, rinse in a colander under cool running water. Trim stems, slice and cook immediately. Do not wash mushrooms until just before you intend to use them.

Eggplant and Cheese Rolls

The basil in the pesto and tomato sauce adds an intriguing taste to this elegant but easy-to-make starter. It will please even your most discriminating guests.

SERVES 6

- PREHEAT OVEN TO 350°F (180°C)
- INDOOR GRILL OR OUTDOOR BARBECUE
- BAKING SHEET, LINED WITH PARCHMENT PAPER

1	large eggplant, sliced lengthwise into 6 long pieces	1
	Salt	
	Olive oil	
1⅓ cups	flaked cooked crab meat, about 7 oz (200 g)	325 mL
¼ cup	ricotta cheese	50 mL
6 tbsp	Classico di Genova Basil Pesto	90 mL
1	jar (26 oz/700 mL) Classico di Napoli Tomato & Basil Pasta Sauce, warmed	1

Variation
Use cooked, chopped salad shrimp in place of the crab meat.

1. Lightly salt eggplant pieces and let stand for 30 minutes. Gently pat off salt and excess moisture.

2. Toss eggplant with oil until coated. Place on grill over medium heat and cook until cooked through, about 2 to 3 minutes per side. Let cool.

3. Combine crab meat with cheese. Place eggplant slices on prepared baking sheet. Spread 1 tbsp (15 mL) pesto evenly over each slice. Top each slice with about 3 tbsp (45 mL) crab mixture and roll, placing seam-side down on baking sheet. Bake in preheated oven for 20 minutes. Serve with warm pasta sauce.

Tip: If an indoor or outdoor barbecue is not available, cook the eggplant in a skillet until just tender.

Garlic Shrimp

This quick sauté of succulent shrimp is a superb finger food for any party. Spear with toothpicks and serve alongside marinated olives and artichokes.

SERVES 6

2 tbsp	olive oil	25 mL
1 lb	large shrimp, peeled and deveined	500 g
4 to 5	cloves garlic, minced	4 to 5
¼ cup	chopped fresh parsley	50 mL
1 cup	Classico di Piemonte Red Wine & Herb Pasta Sauce	250 mL
	Salt and freshly ground black pepper	

1. In a large skillet, heat oil over medium-high heat. Add shrimp and cook for 2 to 3 minutes. Add garlic and parsley. Cook until shrimp is cooked through, about 1 to 2 minutes more. Stir in pasta sauce and heat through. Season with salt and pepper to taste.

Tip: Shrimp cook quite quickly. Shrimp are cooked when they are opaque in the center, pink on the outside and firm to the touch.

White Bean Dip with Lemon

Here's a delicious dip with rich Italian flavors that couldn't be easier to make. For convenience, prepare ahead and spoon into a rustic dish. When you're ready to serve, surround with pita, flat bread or, to continue the Italian theme, crostini. To make crostini, brush thin slices of baguette with olive oil and toast under the broiler until lightly browned, turning once.

SERVES 4

2	cloves garlic, minced	2
1	can (19 oz/540 mL) white kidney beans, drained and rinsed	1
¼ cup	water	50 mL
3 to 4 tbsp	freshly squeezed lemon juice	45 to 60 mL
3 to 4 tbsp	olive oil	45 to 60 mL
3 to 4 tbsp	Classico di Genova Basil Pesto	45 to 60 mL
	Salt and freshly ground black pepper, to taste	

Variation
Substitute the white kidney beans with Romano beans.

1. In a food processor, combine garlic, kidney beans, water, lemon juice, oil and pesto. Process until well combined and smooth. If dip is too thick, add a little water and continue to process until desired consistency. Season with salt and pepper to taste.

Tip: For a little spice, add a pinch of chili powder or finely chopped fresh red chilies to the mixture before processing.

Sun-Dried Tomato Artichoke Dip

This quick and easy dip is a perfect starter or snack. Serve with crackers, tortilla chips or crudités such as carrot sticks or broccoli florets.

SERVES 8 TO 10

- PREHEAT OVEN TO 400°F (200°C)
- 9-INCH (23 CM) PIE PLATE

2	jars (each 6 oz/170 mL) artichoke hearts, drained and chopped	2
1	package (8 oz/ 250 g) cream cheese, softened	1
⅔ cup	Classico di Sardegna Sun-Dried Tomato Pesto	150 mL
½ cup	freshly grated Parmesan cheese	125 mL
⅓ cup	whipping (35%) cream	75 mL

1. In a medium bowl, mix together artichoke hearts, cream cheese, pesto, Parmesan and whipping cream.

2. Spread mixture into pie plate and bake in preheated oven until heated through, about 10 to 15 minutes.

Tip: Make this recipe ahead and store covered in the refrigerator until ready to heat.

Grilled Polenta with Roasted Portobello Mushroom

Polenta is a staple in Italian kitchens, in part because it blends well with many different flavors. This combination of tomatoes, mushrooms and Parmesan is traditional and delicious. It makes a great first course to any dinner. For convenience, prepare the polenta ahead of time, then grill while the sauce is heating.

SERVES 6

• 8-INCH (2 L) SQUARE BAKING DISH, LINED WITH PARCHMENT PAPER
• INDOOR GRILL OR OUTDOOR BARBECUE

4 cups	water	1 L
1 tsp	salt	5 mL
1 cup	cornmeal	250 mL
¼ cup	butter, divided	50 mL
⅓ cup	freshly grated Parmesan cheese	75 mL
1	jar (26 oz/700 mL) Classico di Toscana Portobello Mushroom Pasta Sauce	1

1. In a medium saucepan, bring water and salt to a boil. Gradually stir in cornmeal and half the butter. Cook over low heat, stirring constantly, for 20 minutes. Mixture will become quite thick. Stir in remaining butter and Parmesan cheese. Pour cooked polenta evenly into prepared baking dish. Cool completely, then chill until firm. Slice into 12 wedges.

2. Place polenta wedges on greased grill over medium heat. Cook on both sides until heated through, about 3 to 4 minutes.

3. In the meantime, in a large saucepan, heat pasta sauce. Serve polenta with about 7 tbsp (105 mL) sauce over top.

Tip: Parchment paper is an indispensable item to have in your pantry. It is a nonstick paper that doesn't have to be greased. It also tolerates heat, making it an excellent liner for baking dishes and pans.

Tip: The polenta wedges can be heated in a skillet instead of a grill, if desired.

Tomato Chili Hummus

Here's a flavorful take on hummus, the Mediterranean chickpea dip. This version includes tahini and adds sun-dried tomato pesto for a new twist. Accompany with pita bread triangles.

1	can (19 oz/540 mL) chickpeas, drained and rinsed	1
¼ cup	freshly squeezed lemon juice	50 mL
¼ cup	tahini	50 mL
⅓ cup	water	75 mL
¼ cup	olive oil	50 mL
1 to 2	garlic cloves, minced	1 to 2
3 tbsp	Classico di Sardegna Sun-Dried Tomato Pesto (or to taste)	45 mL
1	small fresh hot red chili pepper, finely chopped	1
Pinch	salt	Pinch

Variation
Substitute the tahini with 1 tbsp (15 mL) sesame oil.

1. In a food processor, combine chickpeas, lemon juice, tahini, water, oil, garlic, pesto, chili pepper and salt. Process until well combined and smooth. If mixture is too thick, add a little water and continue to process until desired consistency. Adjust seasoning, if required.

Brie and Onion Bake

This dish is such a crowd pleaser, you'd be wise to make two. Rich creamy Brie is topped with melt-in-your-mouth caramelized onions and pesto. This inspired combination is then nestled in layers of phyllo and baked until the outside is golden brown and the center is divinely molten.

SERVES 4 TO 6

- PREHEAT OVEN TO 400°F (200°C)
- BAKING SHEET

1/3 cup	butter, divided	75 mL
2 cups	chopped onion, about 4 medium	500 mL
Pinch	salt	Pinch
Pinch	granulated sugar	Pinch
1 tsp	cider vinegar	5 mL
3	sheets phyllo pastry	3
1	4-inch (10 cm) round Brie or Camembert cheese	1
2 tbsp	Classico di Genova Basil Pesto	25 mL

1. In a skillet, melt 2 tbsp (25 mL) butter over medium heat. Add onions, salt and sugar. Reduce heat to medium-low and cook, stirring occasionally, until onions are golden, about 15 to 20 minutes. Set aside.

2. Melt remaining butter. Place one sheet of phyllo on work surface. Cover remaining sheets with plastic wrap and a damp cloth to prevent drying out. Brush phyllo sheet lightly with butter. Top with second sheet. Repeat with remaining phyllo and butter. Trim to make 11-inch (27 cm) square.

3. Place Brie in center of phyllo square. Spread pesto over top. Mound onions over pesto. Fold one corner of phyllo over top of Brie, continue folding and pleating to cover completely. Brush with butter. Place on baking sheet. Bake in preheated oven until golden brown, about 18 to 20 minutes.

Variation

For a last minute Baked Pesto Brie, slice Brie in half horizontally. Spread bottom half with 2 tbsp (25 mL) pesto. Replace top. Place in heatproof serving dish, covered lightly with foil. Bake in 375°F (190°C) oven for 10 to 15 minutes or until cheese is hot and softened.

Soups and Salads

❧

Hearty Vegetable Soup

Hearty Vegetable Soup

When there is a chill in the air, there is nothing like a steaming bowl of soup to warm you up. This version adds plenty of garden vegetables for a nutritious and satisfying soup.

SERVES 4 TO 6

3 tbsp	vegetable oil	45 mL
1	leek, white and light green part only, washed and cut lengthwise and thinly sliced (see Tip, below)	1
1	onion, diced	1
1	carrot, thinly sliced	1
1	stalk celery, sliced	1
1½ cups	chopped cabbage, about 3 large cabbage leaves	375 mL
1	jar (26 oz/700 mL) Classico di Capri Sun-Dried Tomato Pasta Sauce	1
2½ cups	vegetable or chicken stock	625 mL
1½ cups	canned chickpeas	375 mL
	Salt and freshly ground black pepper	

Variation
Substitute chickpeas with lentils.

1. In a large saucepan, heat oil over medium heat. Add leek, onion, carrot, celery and cabbage. Cook, stirring, until the vegetables have softened, about 12 minutes.

2. Stir in pasta sauce and stock. Bring to a boil. Reduce heat to medium-low and simmer, stirring occasionally, for 10 minutes. Add chickpeas and cook for 2 to 3 minutes more. Season with salt and pepper to taste.

Tip: Leeks need a little care when cleaning. Trim the root and cut off the dark green tops. Cut the leek in half lengthwise and wash under cold running water, gently rubbing to loosen the dirt.

Potato and Garlic Soup

This creamy and delicious soup combines the mellow flavors of roasted garlic and potatoes. Pesto adds a flavorful finish.

SERVES 4 TO 6

3 tbsp	butter	45 mL
1	onion, diced	1
3	potatoes, peeled and diced	3
5 cups	chicken or vegetable stock	1.25 L
6	cloves garlic, roasted (see Tip, below)	6
⅓ cup	whipping (35%) cream	75 mL
2 to 3 tbsp	Classico di Genova Basil Pesto	25 to 45 mL
	Salt and freshly ground black pepper	

1. In a large saucepan, melt butter over medium heat. Add onion and potatoes. Cook for 10 to 12 minutes.

2. Add stock and garlic. Bring to boil. Reduce heat to medium-low and simmer, stirring occasionally, until the potatoes are soft, about 15 minutes. Remove from heat.

3. In a food processor, purée soup, in batches, until smooth. Pour puréed soup back into saucepan and place on medium heat. Add cream and cook for 2 to 3 minutes. Stir in pesto. Season with salt and pepper to taste.

Tip: To roast garlic: Trim the top quarter off a head of garlic, exposing the cloves, or peel the skin from individual cloves. Wrap in foil and bake at 400°F (200°C) until the garlic is soft and tender, about 30 minutes.

Sweet Corn, Sausage and Tomato Soup

The addition of corn and fresh basil distinguishes this robust soup. It is so packed with vegetables and Italian sausage that it's really a meal in itself.

SERVES 4 TO 6

2 tbsp	olive oil	25 mL
2	cloves garlic, minced	2
2	new white potatoes, diced	2
1	onion, diced	1
1	red bell pepper, diced	1
1	jar (26 oz/700 mL) Classico Italian Sausage, Peppers & Onions Pasta Sauce	1
3 cups	vegetable or chicken stock	750 mL
1 cup	corn kernels, canned or frozen, thawed, if frozen	250 mL
2 tbsp	chopped fresh basil leaves	25 mL
	Salt and freshly ground black pepper	

Variation
Try an addition of diced carrot or leek for another flavor change.

1. In a large saucepan, heat oil over medium heat. Add garlic, potatoes, onion and red pepper. Cook, stirring occasionally, for 8 to 10 minutes.

2. Stir in pasta sauce and stock. Bring to a boil. Reduce heat to medium-low and simmer, uncovered, for 15 minutes. Add corn and basil. Cook for 1 to 2 minutes more. Season with salt and pepper to taste.

Spicy Two-Bean Soup

Here's a fresh take on that classic Italian combo, pasta and fagioli. This easy-to-make version packs a welcome punch with the addition of a spicy red pepper in the sauce.

SERVES 4 TO 6

2 tbsp	olive oil	25 mL
4	cloves garlic, minced	4
1	onion, diced	1
1	jar (26 oz/700 mL) Classico di Roma Arrabbiata Spicy Red Pepper Pasta Sauce	1
3 cups	chicken stock	750 mL
1 cup	dry small shell pasta	250 mL
1 cup	canned chickpeas, drained and rinsed	250 mL
1 cup	canned white kidney beans, drained and rinsed	250 mL
¼ cup	chopped fresh parsley	50 mL
	Salt and freshly ground black pepper	
	Freshly grated Parmesan cheese, optional	

Variation
Use your favorite short pasta.

1. In a large saucepan, heat oil over medium heat. Add garlic and onion. Cook until vegetables are softened, about 5 to 6 minutes.

2. Stir in pasta sauce and stock. Bring to a boil. Add pasta. Reduce heat to medium-low and simmer, stirring occasionally, until pasta is tender, about 8 minutes.

3. Stir in chickpeas, kidney beans and parsley. Cook for 2 to 3 minutes more. Season with salt and pepper to taste. Sprinkle Parmesan over top, if using.

Romaine and Radicchio Salad with Creamy Pesto Dressing

Don't reserve that jar of basil pesto exclusively for pasta. It is actually a versatile sauce that works very well as an enhancement to salad dressing. Here, it marries with mayonnaise to add a wonderful flavor to a crisp, refreshing salad that pairs well with pasta dishes.

SERVES 4

½ cup	mayonnaise	125 mL
1 tbsp	Classico di Genova Basil Pesto (or to taste)	15 mL
2 to 3 tbsp	freshly squeezed lemon juice	25 to 45 mL
4 to 5	slices smoked bacon	4 to 5
1	head romaine lettuce	1
5 to 6	radicchio lettuce leaves	5 to 6
	Salt and freshly ground black pepper	
	Shaved Parmesan cheese, optional	

1. In a bowl, combine mayonnaise, pesto and lemon juice. Set aside.

2. Chop bacon into 1-inch (2.5 cm) pieces. In a small skillet over medium heat, cook bacon until crisp. Set aside

3. Wash romaine and radicchio and tear into generous bite-size pieces. Toss with reserved mayonnaise-pesto dressing. Season with salt and pepper to taste. Serve topped with bacon and shaved Parmesan, if using.

Tip: Make the dressing a few hours ahead and store, covered, in the refrigerator until ready to use.

Tomato and Bocconcini Cheese Salad

Make an impression with this luscious salad that is as colorful as it is tasty. Serve on chilled glass plates to begin an alfresco dinner in the heat of summer or add crusty Italian bread for a light lunch.

SERVES 4

12 oz	cherry tomatoes, cut in half	375 g
2	pieces bocconcini cheese, cut into 8 wedges	2
2 to 3 tbsp	Classico di Genova Basil Pesto	25 to 45 mL
1 tbsp	apple cider vinegar	15 mL
1 tbsp	olive oil	15 mL
	Salt and freshly ground black pepper	
6 cups	mesclun salad mix	1.5 L

1. In a bowl, toss together tomatoes, cheese, pesto, vinegar and oil. Season with salt and pepper to taste.

2. Divide lettuce evenly among four plates. Top each with the tomato mixture.

Tip: If you can't find mesclun salad mix, make your own by combining delicate greens such as frisée, arugula, oak leaf, baby spinach and radicchio.

Tip: For an eye-catching presentation, use a combination of red and yellow cherry tomatoes.

Potato Salad

Here's a dynamite recipe for potato salad that uses sun-dried tomato pesto to create great flavor. This makes a perfect addition to a Sunday afternoon barbecue.

1½ lbs	mini new red or white potatoes, cut in half	750 g
4 oz	green beans, cut in half	125 g
1 tbsp	olive oil	15 mL
1	onion, finely chopped	1
1	stalk celery, finely chopped	1
6 tbsp	mayonnaise	90 mL
1 to 2 tbsp	Classico di Sardegna Sun-Dried Tomato Pesto	15 to 25 mL
1 tbsp	red wine vinegar	15 mL
	Salt and freshly ground black pepper	

Variation

Substitute the Classico di Sardegna Sun-Dried Tomato Pesto with Classico di Genova Basil Pesto.

1. In a large saucepan, cook unpeeled potatoes in boiling salted water until tender, about 15 to 20 minutes. Add beans during the last 5 minutes of cooking. Drain and reserve.

2. In a skillet, heat oil over medium-high heat. Add onion and celery. Cook, stirring occasionally, until tender. Remove and cool slightly.

3. In a bowl, whisk together mayonnaise, pesto and vinegar. Season with salt and pepper to taste.

4. Toss drained potatoes and green beans with pesto dressing and onion mixture until well combined. Cover and let stand 30 minutes to blend flavors.

Tip: This salad stores well in an airtight container in the refrigerator.

Three-Bean and Corn Salad

Make an effort to find sherry vinegar for this recipe as it has a wonderful flavor. This refreshing and versatile salad, which looks beautiful on a buffet table, also makes an excellent accompaniment to grilled chicken, fish or seafood.

SERVES 4 TO 6

1 cup	canned chickpeas, drained and rinsed	250 mL
1 cup	canned Romano beans, drained and rinsed	250 mL
1 cup	canned black-eyed peas, drained and rinsed	250 mL
1 cup	cooked corn kernels	250 mL
¼ cup	chopped fresh parsley	50 mL
4 to 5 tbsp	Classico di Sardegna Sun-Dried Tomato Pesto	60 to 75 mL
2 tbsp	sherry vinegar	25 mL
3 tbsp	olive oil	45 mL
1	clove garlic, minced	1
	Salt and freshly ground black pepper	

1. In a bowl, combine chickpeas, Romano beans, black-eyed peas, corn, parsley, pesto, vinegar, olive oil and garlic. Season with salt and pepper to taste. Cover and let stand for 30 minutes to blend flavors.

Variations

If you can't find sherry vinegar, you can substitute it with apple cider vinegar.

Try adding finely diced red pepper for another great taste.

Chickpea Salad with Grilled Shrimp

The addition of sun-dried tomato pesto and chili pepper to a traditional vinaigrette transforms simple chickpeas into a splendid salad. Add grilled shrimp and crisp baby spinach for a fabulous dish that can be served as a starter, a side dish or as a main course to follow soup.

SERVES 4

Variation
Substitute the baby spinach with arugula.

• INDOOR GRILL OR OUTDOOR BARBECUE

Salad

1	can (19 oz/540 mL) chickpeas, drained and rinsed	1
2 tbsp	freshly squeezed lemon juice	25 mL
2 tbsp	chopped fresh parsley	25 mL
2 tbsp	olive oil	25 mL
2 tbsp	Classico di Sardegna Sun-Dried Tomato Pesto (or to taste)	25 mL
1 tsp	chopped fresh hot red chili pepper, about ½ a pepper	5 mL
	Salt and freshly ground black pepper	

Grilled Shrimp

¼ cup	freshly squeezed lemon juice	50 mL
2 tbsp	olive oil	25 mL
1 to 2	garlic cloves, minced	1 to 2
1 tbsp	chopped fresh parsley	15 mL
	Salt and freshly ground black pepper	
12	jumbo or large shrimp, peeled and deveined	12
2 cups	baby spinach	500 mL

1. Salad: In a bowl, combine chickpeas, lemon juice, parsley, oil, pesto and chili pepper. Season with salt and pepper to taste. Let stand for 30 minutes to blend flavors.

continued on page 40

2. **Shrimp:** In another bowl, whisk together lemon juice, oil, garlic and parsley. Season with salt and pepper to taste. Pour over shrimp and let stand for 20 minutes.

3. Cook shrimp on a greased grill over medium-high heat until just cooked through, about 3 to 4 minutes per side.

4. Just before serving, combine baby spinach and chickpea mixture. Place on four individual serving dishes and top each with 3 shrimp.

Tip: The shrimp can be cooked on top of the stove. Heat olive oil in a skillet over medium-high heat. Add shrimp and cook until cooked through, about 3 to 4 minutes per side.

Other Great Recipes Featuring
Classico di Sardegna Sun-Dried Tomato Pesto

Appetizers
Spinach, Feta and Sun-Dried Tomato Triangles (*page 14*)
Sun-Dried Tomato Artichoke Dip (*page 21*)

Chicken
Chicken Burgers (*page 126*)

Fish
Baked Cod with Vegetables (*page 148*)

Meat
Pork Tenderloin with Cream Sauce (*page 101*)

Pasta
Fusilli with Eggplant, Olives and Sun-Dried Tomato Pesto (*page 45*)

Vegetables
Roasted Vegetable Spread with Olives and Pesto (*page 163*)

For a complete list of recipes using this sauce,
see Index by Sauce (*page 185*).

Artichoke and Sun-Dried Tomato Salad

Here's an unusual, but tasty salad that takes no time to prepare. Artichokes and cheese are a great combination. Build on this affinity by serving this delicious salad with a savory tart such as Leek, Gruyère and Sun-Dried Tomato Pesto Tart (see recipe, page 160).

SERVES 4

2	cans (each 14 oz/398 mL) artichoke hearts	2
2	green onions, finely chopped	2
2 tbsp	chopped fresh parsley	25 mL
½ tsp	Dijon mustard	2 mL
1 tbsp	red wine vinegar	15 mL
2 tbsp	olive oil	25 mL
3 to 4 tbsp	Classico di Sardegna Sun-Dried Tomato Pesto	45 to 60 mL
	Salt and freshly ground black pepper	

1. Drain and rinse artichoke hearts, then slice in half lengthwise through the base.

2. In a bowl, combine artichoke hearts, green onions and parsley.

3. In another bowl, whisk together Dijon mustard, vinegar, oil and pesto. Season with salt and pepper to taste. Toss with artichoke mixture.

Tip: This salad will keep for up to three days, covered, in the refrigerator.

Pasta

Linguine with Spinach,
Grilled Peppers and Goat Cheese *44*

Fusilli with Eggplant, Olives and
Sun-Dried Tomato Pesto *45*

Fettuccine with Snow Peas and Goat Cheese *46*

Asparagus and Mushrooms Noodles Alfredo *48*

Spaghettini Primavera *49*

Rotini with Mushrooms and Peas *50*

Cheese-Filled Tortellini with Fresh Basil *52*

Fettuccine with Asparagus and Blue Cheese *53*

Fusilli with Artichoke Hearts *54*

Penne with Tomato Cream Vodka Sauce *56*

Rigatoni, Cheese and Pesto Bake *57*

Penne with Leek, Smoked Ham and Asparagus *58*

Cheese Cannelloni *60*

Rigatoni with Ham and Peas *62*

Gnocchi with Chorizo Sausage,
Roasted Pepper and Parsley *64*

Classic Vegetarian Lasagna *66*

Lasagna Florentine *68*

Garlic Alfredo Noodles
with Roasted Red Pepper and Spinach *70*

Creamy Seafood Fettuccine *71*

Spaghettini with Scallops and Tomato Pesto *72*

Penne Rigate with
Smoked Salmon and Green Onions *74*

Spaghetti with Clams and Basil Pesto *75*

Fettuccine with Shrimp and Mussels *76*

Linguine with Spinach, Grilled Peppers and Goat Cheese

Linguine with Spinach, Grilled Peppers and Goat Cheese

Here's another quick combination of vegetables and cheese in a creamy sauce. The goat cheese adds a distinctive finish to the dish.

SERVES 4

12 oz	linguine	375 g
1 tbsp	butter	15 mL
1	small onion, finely chopped	1
4 oz	baby spinach	125 g
½	grilled red bell pepper, diced (see Tip, below)	½
½	grilled yellow bell pepper, diced	½
1	jar (16 oz/435 mL) Classico Alfredo di Capri Sun-Dried Tomato Pasta Sauce	1
2 oz	goat cheese, sliced into rounds	60 g
	Chopped or whole chives, optional	

Variation
Use spaghetti in place of linguine.

1. Cook linguine according to package directions.

2. In a large skillet, melt butter over medium heat. Add onion and cook until softened, about 6 to 7 minutes. Add spinach and cook until just wilted, about 1 minute. Add red and yellow pepper and pasta sauce. Simmer (do not boil), stirring occasionally, about 2 to 3 minutes.

3. Toss linguine with sauce and served topped with goat cheese and chives, if using.

Tip: To grill a pepper: Cut pepper into 3 or 4 large pieces (somewhat resembling wedges). Remove the seeds and membrane. Toss with a little oil and place on greased grill over medium heat. Cook until softened and lightly charred, turning occasionally to prevent burning. Remove from heat and cool.

Fusilli with Eggplant, Olives and Sun-Dried Tomato Pesto

Here's a great dish with an abundance of color and flavor. Add some crusty bread and, if you're feeling festive, red or white wine for a delicious weekday meal.

12 oz	fusilli	375 g
3 tbsp	olive oil (approx.)	45 mL
1	garlic clove, finely chopped	1
1	onion, finely chopped	1
2	baby Italian eggplants, diced	2
3 oz	baby spinach	90 g
½ cup	chicken stock	125 mL
⅓ cup	whole pitted olives (or to taste)	75 mL
4 tbsp	Classico di Sardegna Sun-Dried Tomato Pesto (or to taste)	60 mL
	Salt and freshly ground black pepper	
	Chopped fresh parsley	
	Freshly grated Parmesan cheese	

Variation
Use rotini in place of fusilli.

1. Cook fusilli according to package directions.

2. In a large skillet, heat oil over medium heat. Add garlic, onion and eggplant. Cook until tender, about 6 to 7 minutes, adding more oil if required. Add spinach and cook until just wilted, about 1 minute. Stir in chicken stock and olives. Simmer for 1 to 2 minutes.

3. Toss fusilli with eggplant mixture and pesto. Season with salt and pepper to taste. Top with parsley and Parmesan. Serve immediately.

Fettuccine with Snow Peas and Goat Cheese

This simple but tasty pasta is bursting with flavor and eye appeal. Garlic lovers can add extra roasted garlic just before tossing.

SERVES 4

12 oz	fettuccine	375 g
2 tbsp	olive oil	25 mL
1	onion, finely chopped	1
1 cup	chopped snow peas	250 mL
1	jar (26 oz/700 mL) Classico di Sorrento Roasted Garlic Pasta Sauce	1
	Salt and freshly ground black pepper	
3 oz	goat cheese, crumbled	90 g
	Chopped fresh parsley	

Variation
Use spaghetti in place of fettuccine.

1. Cook fettuccine according to package directions.

2. In a large skillet, heat oil over medium heat. Add onion and cook until softened, about 6 to 7 minutes. Add snow peas and cook for 2 to 3 minutes. Add pasta sauce and simmer, stirring occasionally, about 3 to 4 minutes. Season with salt and pepper to taste.

3. Toss fettuccine with sauce and serve topped with cheese and parsley.

Asparagus and Mushrooms Noodles Alfredo

Alfredo sauce was invented in Rome in the 1920s. The rich combination of butter, cheese and cream is irresistible. In this tasty variation, the classic sauce is enhanced with the addition of grilled mushrooms and asparagus spears and garnished with flavorful prosciutto. For a change, toss with rotini or orecchiette pasta.

SERVES 4

Variation
Use sautéed mushrooms in place of the grilled. Slice mushrooms and sauté in 1 tbsp (15 mL) butter before adding pasta sauce.

• INDOOR GRILL OR OUTDOOR BARBECUE

6 oz	whole button mushrooms	175 g
Pinch	salt	Pinch
1 tbsp	olive oil	15 mL
8 oz	broad egg noodles	250 g
6	asparagus spears, cut into 2-inch (5 cm) pieces	6
1	jar (16 oz/ 435 mL) Classico Alfredo di Roma Pasta Sauce	1
1 to 2 oz	sliced prosciutto, chopped	30 to 60 g
	Chopped fresh parsley, optional	
	Freshly grated Parmesan cheese, optional	

1. Toss mushrooms with salt and olive oil. Place on greased grill over medium heat and cook until tender and lightly charred, turning to prevent burning, about 8 to 10 minutes. Remove and cool. Chop into small or medium-size pieces.

2. Cook noodles according to package directions, adding asparagus during the last 3 minutes (see Tip, page 53).

3. In a large skillet over medium heat, combine mushrooms and pasta sauce. Simmer (do not boil), stirring occasionally, about 2 to 3 minutes.

4. Toss noodles and asparagus with sauce. Serve topped with prosciutto, parsley and Parmesan cheese, if using.

Tip: Prosciutto is an air-dried and salt-cured ham, which has been aged. This results in a ham that is rich in flavor with a hint of saltiness.

Spaghettini Primavera

Don't save this dish for the vegetarians in your circle, although they will love it, too. This delicious pasta is full of fresh grilled vegetables in a creamy sauce, a fabulous dish when local produce is in season.

SERVES 4 TO 6

• INDOOR GRILL OR OUTDOOR BARBECUE

8 to 12	asparagus spears, trimmed	8 to 12
1	red bell pepper, cut into 3 to 4 large pieces	1
1	zucchini, cut into 3 to 4 long slices	1
Pinch	salt	Pinch
2 tbsp	olive oil, divided	15 mL
1 lb	spaghettini	500 g
2 to 3	green onions, finely chopped	2 to 3
1	jar (26 oz/700 mL) Classico di Toscana Portobello Mushroom Pasta Sauce	1
⅓ cup	whipping (35%) cream	75 mL
	Salt and freshly ground black pepper	
4 to 6 tbsp	crumbled goat cheese	60 to 90 mL

Variation
Use linguine or fettuccine in place of spaghettini.

1. Toss asparagus, red pepper and zucchini with salt and 1 tbsp (15 ml) olive oil. Place vegetables on greased grill over medium heat and cook until just tender and lightly charred, turning to prevent burning, about 6 to 8 minutes. Remove and cool. Slice asparagus into 2-inch (5 cm) pieces and dice the pepper and zucchini.

2. Cook spaghettini according to package directions.

3. In a large skillet, heat remaining oil over medium heat. Add green onions and cook until softened, about 1 to 2 minutes. Stir in pasta sauce, cream, asparagus, bell pepper and zucchini. Simmer, stirring occasionally, about 4 to 5 minutes. Season with salt and pepper to taste.

4. Toss spaghettini with sauce and serve topped with cheese.

Rotini with Mushrooms and Peas

This tasty combination of peas, mushrooms and roasted garlic in a creamy sauce makes a terrific main course for vegetarians. Add some sliced portobello mushrooms to the mix to provide the illusion of heartiness.

SERVES 4

12 oz	rotini	375 g
2 tbsp	butter	25 mL
1 lb	assorted mushrooms, sliced	500 g
1 cup	frozen green peas, thawed	250 mL
2 tbsp	finely chopped fresh parsley	25 mL
1	jar (16 oz/435 mL) Classico Alfredo di Sorrento Roasted Garlic Pasta Sauce	1

1. Cook rotini according to package directions.

2. In a large skillet, melt butter over medium heat. Add mushrooms and cook until tender, about 5 to 6 minutes. Add peas, parsley and pasta sauce. Simmer (do not boil), stirring occasionally, about 2 to 3 minutes.

3. Toss rotini with sauce and serve topped with additional parsley, if desired.

Variation
Use penne rigate in place of rotini.

Cheese-Filled Tortellini with Fresh Basil

This dish is so easy to prepare. Cheese-filled tortellini is tossed with a simple, but delicious pancetta-based sauce, which is finished with fresh basil.

1 lb	fresh cheese-filled tortellini	500 g
1 tbsp	olive oil	15 mL
4 oz	pancetta, diced (see Tip, below)	125 g
1	onion, finely chopped	1
¼ tsp	hot pepper flakes (or to taste)	1 mL
1	jar (26 oz/700 mL) Classico di Piemonte Red Wine & Herb Pasta Sauce	1
¼ cup	chopped fresh basil	50 mL
	Salt and freshly ground black pepper	
	Freshly grated Romano or Parmesan cheese	

Variations

Substitute pancetta with smoked bacon.

Stir in ½ cup (125 mL) cooked green peas.

Frozen cheese-filled tortellini work just as well.

1. Cook tortellini according to package directions.

2. In a large skillet, heat oil over medium heat. Add pancetta and cook for 2 to 3 minutes. Add onion and hot pepper flakes. Cook until the onion is softened, about 6 to 7 minutes. Stir in pasta sauce and simmer, stirring occasionally, about 3 to 4 minutes. Add basil and simmer for 1 to 2 minutes more. Season with salt and pepper to taste.

3. Toss tortellini with sauce and serve topped with cheese.

Tip: Pancetta comes from the same cut of pork as bacon, but is cured with salt and air-dried and not smoked. It is much firmer than bacon. Look for it in your local grocery store or specialty shop at the deli counter.

Fettuccine with Asparagus and Blue Cheese

This delicious recipe works equally well as a starter or a main course. The blue cheese adds a distinctive touch, but if it is not to your liking, use a milder-tasting cheese, such as Fontina, instead.

SERVES 4

12 oz	fettuccine	375 g
2 tbsp	butter	25 mL
¾ cup	thinly sliced red onion, about 1 small	175 mL
8	asparagus spears, cut into 2-inch (5 cm) pieces	8
1	jar (16 oz/435 mL) Classico Alfredo di Sorrento Roasted Garlic Pasta Sauce	1
⅓ cup	crumbled blue cheese	75 mL

Variation
Try adding a handful of sliced snow peas in place of the asparagus.

1. Cook fettuccine according to package directions, adding asparagus during the last 3 minutes (see Tip, below).

2. In a large skillet, melt butter over medium heat. Add onion and cook until softened, about 6 to 7 minutes. Add asparagus and pasta sauce. Simmer (do not boil), stirring occasionally, about 2 to 3 minutes.

3. Toss fettuccine with sauce. Serve topped with cheese.

Tip: To cook asparagus: Trim bottom and, using a vegetable peeler, peel up to 3 inches (7.5 cm) of the stalk to remove the thick outer layer. Very slender stalks do not need to be peeled. Bring water to a boil in a saucepan, add whole or chopped asparagus and cook until tender-crisp, about 2 to 3 minutes. Drain and rinse.

Fusilli with Artichoke Hearts

This dish is particularly delicious with abundant amounts of Parmesan heaped on top. Treat yourself to good cheese — authentic Parmigiano-Reggiano from the Emilia Romagna region of Italy — and shave it thinly with a cheese shaver, which is available at better kitchen supply stores. You'll be amazed at the difference!

SERVES 4

12 oz	fusilli	375 g
2 tbsp	olive oil	25 mL
1	onion, finely chopped	1
8 oz	mushrooms, sliced	250 g
1	can (14 oz/398 mL) artichoke hearts, drained and quartered	1
1	jar (26 oz/700 mL) Classico di Piemonte Red Wine & Herb Pasta Sauce	1
¼ cup	chopped fresh parsley	50 mL
	Salt and freshly ground black pepper	
	Freshly grated Parmesan or Romano cheese	

Variation
Rigatoni would be a terrific substitution for the fusilli.

1. Cook fusilli according to package directions.

2. In a large skillet, heat oil over medium heat. Add onion and mushrooms. Cook until vegetables are tender, about 6 to 7 minutes. Add artichoke hearts, pasta sauce and parsley. Simmer, stirring occasionally, about 4 to 5 minutes. Season with salt and pepper to taste.

3. Toss fusilli with sauce and serve topped with cheese.

Penne with Tomato Cream Vodka Sauce

Pasta tossed with a vodka-enhanced tomato sauce has become a classic and not without reason. Vodka seems to complement the tomatoes and the addition of cream makes this version a real winner.

SERVES 4 TO 6

1 lb	penne rigate	500 g
4 to 5	slices bacon, finely chopped	4 to 5
1	onion, finely chopped	1
⅓ cup	vodka	75 mL
1	jar (26 oz/700 mL) Classico di Napoli Tomato & Basil Pasta Sauce	1
⅓ cup	whipping (35%) cream	75 mL
¼ cup	chopped fresh parsley	50 mL

Variation
Substitute chicken broth for vodka.

1. Cook penne rigate according to package directions.

2. In a large skillet over medium heat, cook bacon for 2 to 3 minutes. Add onion and cook until softened and the bacon is just crisp. Add vodka and cook until most of the vodka has evaporated, about 1 minute. Stir in pasta sauce and cream. Simmer, stirring occasionally, about 4 to 5 minutes.

3. Toss penne rigate with sauce and parsley. Serve immediately.

Tip: Penne is available either smooth or ridged. Penne lisce has a smooth surface while penne rigate is ridged. Use either in this dish.

Rigatoni, Cheese and Pesto Bake

Here's a terrific recipe that combines meat, pasta and cheese and is certain to become a family favorite. Just add crusty Italian bread and a tossed green salad for a delicious and nutritious meal.

SERVES 8

- PREHEAT OVEN TO 350°F (180°C)
- 13-BY 9-INCH (3 L) BAKING DISH

1 lb	rigatoni	500 g
1 lb	lean ground beef	500 g
2	jars (each 26 oz/700 mL) Classico di Genoa Tomato & Pesto Pasta Sauce	2
2 cups	ricotta cheese	500 mL
4 cups	shredded mozzarella cheese	1 L
¼ cup	freshly grated Parmesan cheese	50 mL
2	eggs, beaten	2

1. Cook rigatoni according to package directions.

2. In a large skillet over medium-high heat, brown beef. Drain fat from pan. Reduce heat to medium. Stir in pasta sauce and simmer, stirring occasionally, for 10 minutes. Remove from heat.

3. Combine ricotta cheese, 1 cup (250 mL) mozzarella cheese, Parmesan and eggs. Spread 1½ cups (375 mL) sauce in baking dish. Top with half each of the cooked rigatoni, ricotta cheese mixture and sauce. Sprinkle with 1 cup (250 mL) mozzarella cheese. Repeat layering, ending with sauce. Top with remaining cheese. Bake, uncovered, in preheated oven until hot and bubbly, about 40 to 45 minutes. Let stand 10 minutes before serving.

Tip: Convert this dish to a vegetarian casserole by replacing the beef with 2 to 3 cups (500 to 750 mL) chopped assorted roasted or grilled vegetables. To roast vegetables, see Tip, page 154.

Penne with Leek, Smoked Ham and Asparagus

Here's a tasty recipe to make when fresh asparagus is in season. The delicate flavor of shallots and leeks marries well with the stronger tastes of the smoked ham and sun-dried tomatoes. The creamy sauce and crisp asparagus pull all the ingredients together. A great dish for an elegant main course.

SERVES 4

12 oz	penne rigate	375 g
2 tbsp	butter	25 mL
1	shallot, finely chopped	1
1	leek, light green and white part only, washed and finely chopped (see Tip, page 28)	1
10	asparagus spears, steamed or grilled, sliced on the diagonal (see Tip, page 53)	10
6 oz	smoked ham, cut into thin matchstick strips	175 g
1	jar (16 oz/435 mL) Classico Alfredo di Capri Sun-Dried Tomato Pasta Sauce	1
	Salt and freshly ground black pepper	
1 tbsp	chopped fresh parsley or rosemary, optional	15 mL

1. Cook penne according to package directions.

2. In a skillet, melt butter over medium heat. Add shallot and leek. Cook until tender, about 6 to7 minutes. Add asparagus, ham and pasta sauce. Simmer (do not boil), stirring occasionally, about 2 to 3 minutes. Season with salt and pepper to taste.

3. Toss penne with sauce and parsley, if using. Serve immediately.

Variation

Try adding a handful of sliced snow peas in place of the asparagus.

Cheese Cannelloni

This creamy cannelloni will certainly appeal to vegetarians, but others will also enjoy its velvety charm. Add hot Italian bread and steamed broccoli or a tossed salad for a nutritious, comforting meal.

SERVES 4 TO 6

- PREHEAT OVEN TO 350°C (180°F)
- 13-BY 9-INCH (3 L) BAKING DISH

1 tbsp	olive oil	15 mL
½ cup	finely chopped onion, about 1 medium	125 mL
½ cup	finely chopped red bell pepper, about ½ a pepper	125 mL
½ cup	finely chopped celery, about 1 stalk	125 mL
2	cloves garlic, minced	2
½ tsp	salt	2 mL
½ tsp	dried parsley leaves	2 mL
1	egg, beaten	1
1 cup	ricotta cheese	250 mL
¼ cup	freshly grated Parmesan or Romano Cheese	50 mL
1	jar (26 oz/700 mL) Classico di Parma Four Cheese Pasta Sauce	1
12	no-boil cannelloni	12
1 cup	water	250 mL
	Freshly grated Parmesan cheese	

1. In a large skillet, heat oil over medium heat. Add onion, red pepper, celery, garlic, salt and parsley. Cook until vegetables are tender, about 7 to 8 minutes. Remove from heat and cool. Stir in egg, ricotta and Parmesan until well combined.

2. Spread half of the pasta sauce in baking dish. Fill cannelloni with cheese mixture and place in single layer over sauce. Cover with remaining sauce. Drizzle water over all.

3. Bake, covered, in preheated oven until cannelloni are tender, about 50 to 55 minutes. Serve topped with Parmesan cheese.

....

Tip: This recipe can be baked, cooled and frozen. Portion and freeze for up to 2 months in microwave-safe containers with lids or in oven-to-freezer-safe baking dishes covered with foil. To reheat, simply thaw in the refrigerator and heat in a 325°F (160°C) oven for about 30 minutes or in a microwave oven on medium power for 3 to 4 minutes or until warmed through.

Other Great Recipes Featuring
Classico di Parma Four Cheese Pasta Sauce

Chicken
Cheese-Crusted Chicken Breasts (*page 128*)

Vegetables
Creamy Mushroom Risotto (*page 164*)
Layered Eggplant Casserole (*page 153*)

For a complete list of recipes using this sauce, see Index by Sauce (*page 185*).

Rigatoni with Ham and Peas

Great with a crisp salad, this fast pasta is sure to become a staple for busy weeknights. If you crave spice or just feel the need for variety, add finely chopped chili pepper, to taste, just before serving.

SERVES 4

12 oz	rigatoni	375 g
2 tbsp	olive oil	25 mL
3	green onions, chopped	3
4 oz	smoked ham, diced	125 g
1 cup	frozen green peas, thawed	250 mL
1	jar (26 oz/700 mL) Classico di Parma Four Cheese Pasta Sauce	1
3 tbsp	chopped fresh parsley or basil leaves	45 mL
	Salt and freshly ground black pepper	

Variation
Substitute the rigatoni with penne.

1. Cook rigatoni according to package directions.

2. In a large skillet, heat oil over medium heat. Add green onions and cook until softened, about 1 to 2 minutes. Add ham, peas and pasta sauce. Simmer, stirring occasionally, about 4 to 5 minutes.

3. Toss rigatoni with sauce and parsley. Season with salt and pepper to taste.

Tip: Add a little whipping cream to make this sauce very creamy.

Gnocchi with Chorizo Sausage, Roasted Pepper and Parsley

Gnocchi are Italian dumplings which, like pasta, are usually served with a savory sauce. In this recipe, chorizo, a highly seasoned sausage, is balanced with creamy Alfredo sauce. The resulting dish is flavorful and delicious. If you can't find chorizo, use spicy Italian sausage instead.

SERVES 4

12 oz	gnocchi	375 g
2	soft chorizo sausages, casing removed	2
1	shallot, finely chopped	1
3 to 4	green onions, chopped	3 to 4
1	jar (16 oz/435 mL) Classico Alfredo di Roma Pasta Sauce	1
1	grilled or roasted red bell pepper, chopped (see Tip, page 44)	1
	Salt and freshly ground black pepper	
	Chopped fresh parsley	

1. Cook gnocchi according to package directions.

2. In a large skillet over medium heat, crumble sausages and cook until no longer pink, about 6 to 7 minutes. Add shallot and green onions. Cook until softened, about 1 to 2 minutes. Add pasta sauce and red pepper. Simmer (do not boil), stirring occasionally, about 2 to 3 minutes. Season with salt and pepper to taste.

3. Toss gnocchi with sauce and serve topped with parsley.

Classic Vegetarian Lasagna

Not for vegetarians only, this delicious lasagna showcases four different cheeses, from mild ricotta to full-flavored feta. The addition of spinach and a spicy red pepper sauce makes it a complete and satisfying meal — just add salad.

SERVE 8

- PREHEAT OVEN TO 350°F (180°C)
- 13-BY 9-INCH (3 L) BAKING DISH

12	lasagna noodles	12
1 tbsp	olive oil	15 mL
1	onion, finely diced	1
1	red bell pepper, finely diced	1
1	jar (26 oz/ 700 mL) Classico di Roma Arrabbiata Spicy Red Pepper Pasta Sauce	1
	Salt and freshly ground black pepper	
1	package (10 oz/300 g) frozen chopped spinach, thawed and well-drained	1
1 lb	ricotta cheese	500 g
1 cup	crumbled feta cheese	250 mL
1/3 cup	freshly grated Parmesan cheese	75 mL
1	egg, beaten	1
1 1/4 cups	freshly grated mozzarella cheese	300 mL

Variation
Substitute cottage cheese for the ricotta.

1. Cook noodles according to package directions.

2. In a large skillet, heat oil over medium heat. Add onion and red pepper. Cook until tender, about 6 to 7 minutes. Stir in pasta sauce and cook until heated through, about 2 to 3 minutes. Season with salt and pepper to taste.

3. Mix together spinach, ricotta, feta, Parmesan and egg.

4. Spoon one-quarter of pasta sauce in baking dish. Top with 3 lasagna noodles, one-quarter of sauce and 3 more noodles. Spread cheese mixture over noodles. Top with 3 more noodles, one-quarter of sauce, remaining noodles and sauce. Sprinkle mozzarella cheese over top. Cover and bake in preheated oven until cooked through, about 40 to 45 minutes. Let stand 10 minutes before serving.

Tip: For those who love meat lasagna, add 12 oz (375 g) ground beef and cook until no longer pink before adding the pasta sauce.

Other Great Recipes Featuring
Classico di Roma Arrabbiata
Spicy Red Pepper Pasta Sauce

Chicken
Chicken Enchiladas (*page 115*)

Soup
Spicy Two-Bean Soup (*page 32*)

For a complete list of recipes using this sauce, see Index by Sauce (*page 185*).

Lasagna Florentine

If you are always on the lookout for a great casserole to bring to the next potluck, look no further. This lasagna is also a family favorite. All it needs is a big salad and some hot crusty rolls.

SERVES 8

- PREHEAT OVEN TO 350°F (180°C)
- 13-BY 9-INCH (3 L) BAKING DISH

2 tbsp	olive oil	25 mL
2	cloves garlic, finely chopped	2
1	onion, finely chopped	1
1	jar (26 oz/700 mL) Classico di Firenze Florentine Spinach & Cheese Pasta Sauce	1
2 cups	ricotta cheese	500 mL
1	egg, beaten	1
Pinch	salt	Pinch
12	cooked lasagna noodles	12
2 cups	shredded mozzarella cheese	500 mL
¼ cup	freshly grated Parmesan cheese	50 mL

Variation
Substitute ricotta cheese with cottage cheese.

1. In a large skillet, heat oil over medium heat. Add garlic and onion. Cook until softened, about 6 to 7 minutes. Stir in pasta sauce and cook until heated through, about 2 to 3 minutes.

2. In a bowl, combine ricotta cheese, egg and salt.

3. Spread one-quarter of sauce in baking dish. Top with 3 lasagna noodles, another one-quarter of sauce and 3 more noodles. Spread ricotta mixture over noodles. Top with 1 cup (250 mL) mozzarella cheese and half of Parmesan cheese. Top with 3 more noodles and one-quarter of sauce. Cover with remaining noodles and sauce. Sprinkle top with remaining Parmesan and mozzarella cheeses. Cover and bake in preheated oven for 35 to 40 minutes. Let stand at least 10 minutes before serving.

Tip: Both extra smooth and regular ricotta cheese work well in this dish.

Garlic Alfredo Noodles with Roasted Red Pepper and Spinach

If you like creamy pasta, you'll love this quick and easy recipe. If you don't have time to roast a pepper, use good-quality bottled roasted peppers instead.

8 oz	broad egg noodles	250 g
1 tbsp	butter	15 mL
1	onion, finely chopped	1
4 oz	fresh spinach, chopped	125 g
½	roasted red bell pepper, diced (see Tip, below)	½
1	jar (16 oz/435 mL) Classico Alfredo di Sorrento Roasted Garlic Pasta Sauce	1
	Freshly grated Asiago or Parmesan cheese, optional	

Variation
Use ½ cup (125 mL) chopped thawed frozen spinach in place of fresh.

1. Cook noodles according to package directions.

2. In a skillet, melt butter over medium heat. Add onion and cook until softened, about 6 to 7 minutes. Add spinach and red pepper. Cook until spinach just wilts, about 1 minute. Stir in pasta sauce. Simmer (do not boil), stirring occasionally, about 2 to 3 minutes.

3. Toss noodles with sauce and serve topped with cheese, if using.

Tip: To roast a pepper: Place pepper over an open gas or charcoal flame or place under a broiler. Turn often until all sides are blackened. Cool then scrape or gently peel away any black bits of skin. Remove seeds and membrane.

Creamy Seafood Fettuccine

Here's a great variation on Fettuccine Alfredo. The rich and decadent sauce is enhanced with the addition of a medley of seafood as well as vegetables, herbs, white wine and lemon juice. This dish is very simple to make, yet impressive enough to serve to the most discriminating guests.

SERVES 4

12 oz	fettuccine	375 g
2 tbsp	butter	25 mL
1	onion, finely diced	1
1	leek, light green and white part only, washed and finely chopped	1
12	mussels, cleaned (see Tip, page 182)	12
12	small clams, such as Manila (see Tip, page 75)	12
1/3 cup	dry white wine or chicken stock	75 mL
12	large shrimp, peeled and deveined	12
1	jar (16 oz/435 mL) Classico Alfredo di Roma Pasta Sauce	1
1/4 cup	freshly squeezed lemon juice, optional	50 mL
2 to 3 tbsp	chopped fresh parsley	25 to 45 mL
	Salt and freshly ground black pepper	

Variation
Chopped fresh chives would be a good substitute for parsley.

1. Cook fettuccine according to package directions.

2. In a large skillet, melt butter over medium heat. Add onion and leek. Cook until softened, about 6 to 7 minutes. Add mussels, clams and wine. Cover and simmer for 3 minutes. Add shrimp and simmer, covered, about 3 to 4 minutes or until mussels and clams open and shrimp are just cooked through and turn pink. Stir in pasta sauce, lemon juice, if using, and parsley. Simmer (do not boil), stirring occasionally, about 2 to 3 minutes. Season with salt and pepper to taste.

3. Serve fettuccine topped with seafood sauce. Serve immediately.

Spaghettini with Scallops and Tomato Pesto

Here's a quick and elegant dish that combines sweet, succulent scallops with asparagus spears and roasted pepper in a tomato and pesto sauce. Add a crisp green salad and cold white wine for a celebratory meal.

SERVES 4

12 oz	spaghettini	375 g
1 tbsp	olive oil	15 mL
1	onion, finely chopped	1
1	jar (26 oz/700 mL) Classico di Genoa Tomato & Pesto Pasta Sauce	1
8 to 12	steamed or grilled asparagus spears, sliced on the diagonal (see Tip, page 53)	8 to 12
1	roasted yellow or red bell pepper, diced (see Tip, page 70)	1
	Salt and freshly ground black pepper	
12	large sea scallops	12
2 tbsp	butter (approx.)	25 mL
	Chopped fresh parsley	

1. Cook spaghettini according to package directions.

2. In a large skillet, heat oil over medium heat. Add onion and cook until softened, about 6 to 7 minutes. Stir in pasta sauce, asparagus and yellow pepper. Simmer, stirring occasionally, about 4 to 5 minutes. Season with salt and pepper to taste.

3. Season scallops with salt and pepper. In another skillet, melt 2 tbsp (25 mL) butter over medium-high heat. Add scallops and cook 30 seconds to 1 minute per side or until just cooked through, adding more butter, if required.

4. Toss spaghettini with sauce and serve topped with scallops and parsley.

Tip: If sea scallops are not available, choose bay scallops and increase the amount to six or seven per person.

Penne Rigate with Smoked Salmon and Green Onions

A flavorful cream sauce, accented with smoked salmon, makes a lovely topping for pasta. This version adds sun-dried tomatoes and green onions for a great finish.

SERVES 4

12 oz	penne rigate	375 g
1 tbsp	butter	15 mL
4	green onions, thinly sliced on the diagonal	4
1	jar (16 oz/435 mL) Classico Alfredo di Capri Sun-Dried Tomato Pasta Sauce	1
4 oz	sliced smoked salmon, cut into strips	125 g
	Chopped chives or parsley, optional	

1. Cook penne rigate according to package directions.

2. In a large skillet, melt butter over medium heat. Add green onions and cook until softened, about 1 to 2 minutes. Stir in pasta sauce and simmer (do not boil), stirring occasionally, about 2 to 3 minutes.

3. Toss penne rigate with sauce and serve topped with salmon and chives, if using.

Variation
Prosciutto would be a great substitution for the salmon.

Spaghetti with Clams and Basil Pesto

Fresh clams, cooked with white wine and herbs, then served over steaming spaghetti, is an Italian classic. And no wonder — the combination is mouth-watering. This version adds basil pesto for an inventive variation.

SERVES 4

12 oz	spaghetti	375 g
1 tbsp	olive oil	15 mL
4 oz	smoked bacon, chopped	125 g
1	onion, finely chopped	1
¼ cup	dry white wine	50 mL
¼ cup	chicken stock	50 mL
1 tsp	finely chopped hot red chili pepper	5 mL
24	small clams, such as Manila (see Tip, below)	24
⅓ cup	Classico di Genova Basil Pesto (or to taste)	75 mL
	Salt and freshly ground black pepper	

Variation

Use canned clams in place of fresh.

1. Cook spaghetti according to package directions.

2. In a large skillet, heat oil over medium heat. Add bacon and onion. Cook until bacon is crisp and onion is softened, about 6 to 7 minutes. Add wine, stock, chili pepper and clams. Cover and simmer until clams open, about 5 to 6 minutes. Discard any clams that do not open.

3. Toss hot spaghetti with clam sauce. Stir in pesto. Season with salt and pepper to taste. Serve immediately.

Tip: Manila clams, sometimes called Japanese clams, are small in size, about 1 inch (2.5 cm) wide, and cook very quickly, making them perfect to use in pasta dishes. If you can't find Manila clams, use littleneck clams instead.

Tip: When buying clams, make sure the shells are tightly closed. If a shell is slightly open, tap it lightly and, if the shell does not close, discard it. Store fresh clams in the refrigerator in a bowl, covered with a damp cloth.

Fettuccine with Shrimp and Mussels

Here's a perfect combination — tender fettuccine is tossed with succulent shrimp and mussels in a spicy red pepper sauce. Accompany with a first course of vegetable soup for a great meal.

SERVES 4

12 oz	fettuccine	375 g
2 tbsp	olive oil	25 mL
8 oz	large shrimp, peeled and deveined	250 g
3	cloves garlic, minced	3
1	onion, finely chopped	1
½ cup	dry white wine	125 mL
1	jar (26 oz/700 mL) Classico di Roma Arrabbiata Spicy Red Pepper Pasta Sauce	1
1 lb	mussels, cleaned (see Tip, page 182)	500 g
¼ cup	chopped fresh parsley	50 mL
	Salt and freshly ground black pepper	
	Additional chopped fresh parsley, optional	

1. Cook fettuccine according to package directions.

2. In a large saucepan, heat oil over medium-high heat. Add shrimp and cook until they turn pink, about 3 to 4 minutes. Remove shrimp and set aside. Reduce heat to medium. Add garlic and onion to saucepan. Cook until softened, about 6 to 7 minutes. Add wine and cook until most of the wine has evaporated. Add pasta sauce and mussels. Cover and simmer until mussels open, about 5 to 7 minutes. Discard any mussels that do not open. Return shrimp and heat through. Stir in parsley and season with salt and pepper to taste.

3. Toss fettuccine with seafood sauce and served topped with additional parsley, if using.

Tip: Buy mussels with tightly closed shells or those that close when lightly tapped, and avoid mussels with broken or cracked shells.

Meat

Beef Chili *80*

Sausage, Pepper and Tomato Toss *81*

Cabbage Rolls *82*

Hearty Pork Stew *85*

Home-Style Beef Stew *86*

Pork Chops with Peppers *89*

Rice and Beef-Stuffed Peppers *90*

Braised Short Ribs *92*

Stuffed Pork Tenderloin with Mushrooms *94*

Sun-Dried Tomato Pesto
and Cheese-Stuffed Pork Chops *97*

Braised Veal Shank *98*

Pork Tenderloin with Cream Sauce *101*

Roast Leg of Lamb
with Tomato, Artichoke and Peppers *102*

Siena Lamb Chops *104*

Fire-Roasted Sauce *106*

Easy Pot Roast *107*

Beef Chili

Beef Chili

If you have a hungry bunch to feed, here's a hearty chili that fits the bill. Succulent chunks of beef are complemented by bits of bacon, flavorful sausage and nutritious beans. Zesty seasonings and a robust sauce complete the mix. Garnish with chopped green onions and sour cream and serve hot onion buns on the side.

SERVES 4 TO 6

1 tbsp	olive oil	15 mL
4	strips bacon, diced (see Tip, below)	4
1½ lbs	boneless lean stewing beef, cut into 1-inch (2.5 cm) cubes	750 g
1 lb	hot or mild Italian sausages, casings removed	500 g
2	onions, diced	2
4	garlic cloves, minced	4
2 tsp	chili powder	10 mL
1 tsp	hot pepper flakes	5 mL
1 tsp	salt	5 mL
1	jar (26 oz/700 mL) Classico Italian Sausage, Peppers & Onions Pasta Sauce	1
1 cup	water	250 mL
1	can (19 oz/540 mL) red kidney beans, drained and rinsed	1

1. In a large heavy saucepan, heat oil over medium heat. Add bacon and cook until just crisp. Remove and set aside.

2. Add beef to saucepan, in batches, and brown on all sides. Crumble sausage and add to pan. Cook for 4 to 5 minutes. Remove and reserve.

3. Add onions, garlic, chili powder, hot pepper flakes and salt. Cook and stir until tender, adding a little water if pan becomes too dry.

4. Stir in pasta sauce, water, reserved meat and bacon. Bring to a boil. Cover and simmer for 1½ hours. Stir in kidney beans and cook for 15 minutes more.

Tip: To make dicing bacon a simple task, place slices on a plate in the freezer. Let stand until firm. Then remove and cut as required in the recipe.

Sausage, Pepper and Tomato Toss

The combination of spicy sausages and sweet peppers in pasta sauce is a marriage made in heaven. Although this dish is very tasty when accompanied by plain white rice, to continue the Italian theme, ladle the sauce over hot, creamy polenta. Add your favorite salad and, if you're feeling festive, open a bottle of Chianti.

1 tbsp	olive oil	15 mL
4	hot Italian sausages	4
1/3 cup	dry white wine	75 mL
4	cloves garlic, minced	4
1	red onion, thinly sliced	1
1	yellow bell pepper, sliced	1
1	green bell pepper, sliced	1
1 1/3 cups	Classico di Firenze Florentine Spinach & Cheese Pasta Sauce	325 mL
1/2 tsp	dried oregano leaves	2 mL
	Salt and freshly ground black pepper	

Variation
Replace the hot sausage with mild for a more mellow taste.

1. In a large deep saucepan, heat oil. Prick sausages with a fork and add to saucepan. Cook over medium-high heat, turning occasionally, until browned. Remove sausages.

2. Add wine to saucepan. Cook and stir until most of wine has evaporated. Add garlic, onion and peppers. Cook until the vegetables are tender, about 6 to 7 minutes. Stir in pasta sauce and oregano. Place sausages over sauce. Bring to a boil and reduce heat. Simmer, covered, for 15 to 20 minutes. Season with salt and pepper to taste. Serve over rice or creamy polenta.

Cabbage Rolls

Not only is this perennial favorite a great dish for a potluck, buffet dinner or a family meal, you'll love the aromas that fill the kitchen as it bakes. Try to find Italian or flat-leaf parsley as it has a more robust flavor than the curly variety and will be a better match for the strongly flavored cabbage.

SERVES 6

- PREHEAT OVEN TO 375°F (190°C)
- 20-CUP (5 L) BAKING CASSEROLE WITH LID

12	large Savoy cabbage leaves	12
1 tsp	olive oil	5 mL
½	onion, finely chopped	½
8 oz	lean ground pork	250 g
3 cups	cooked rice, about 1 cup (250 mL) dry	750 mL
¼ cup	chopped fresh parsley	50 mL
1	jar (26 oz/700 mL) Classico di Sorrento Roasted Garlic Pasta Sauce	1
6 tbsp	freshly grated Romano or Parmesan cheese	90 mL
	Salt and freshly ground black pepper	
1	egg, beaten	1
⅔ cup	water	150 mL

1. In a large saucepan, bring at least 16 cups (4 L) water to a boil. Immerse cabbage leaves into boiling water. Cook until soft enough to fold, about 5 to 6 minutes. Drain and rinse in cold water to cool. Pat dry.

2. In a skillet over medium heat, heat oil. Add onion and cook for 4 to 5 minutes. Add pork and cook until no longer pink. Remove from heat and cool.

continued on page 84

Variations

Green cabbage can be substituted for the Savoy cabbage.

Instead of pork, substitute 2 Italian sausages, removed from casings and crumbled.

3. In a large bowl, combine rice, pork-onion mixture, parsley, 1/3 cup (75 mL) pasta sauce and Romano cheese. Season with salt and pepper to taste. Add egg and mix well. Place about 1/3 cup (75 mL) rice mixture onto bottom of each cabbage leaf. Fold sides inward and roll from base to form a closed packet.

4. Spread half the remaining pasta sauce in baking casserole. Lay cabbage rolls on top of sauce. Spoon remaining sauce over rolls. Drizzle water over top. Cover and bake in preheated oven for 1 hour.

Tip: Choose cabbage that is firm to the touch with tight fresh crisp leaves.

Other Great Recipes Featuring
Classico di Sorrento Roasted Garlic Pasta Sauce

Meat
Roast Leg of Lamb with Tomato, Artichoke and Peppers (*page 102*)

Pasta
Fettuccine with Snow Peas and Goat Cheese (*page 46*)

For a complete list of recipes using this sauce,
see Index by Sauce (*page 185*).

Hearty Pork Stew

Pork is an excellent alternative to beef when making stew. This delicious version has subtle notes of cloves and is so easy to prepare it will soon become a family favorite.

SERVES 4 TO 6

3 lbs	boneless lean stewing pork, cut into 1½-inch (4 cm) cubes	1.5 kg
	Salt and freshly ground black pepper	
2 tbsp	olive oil (approx.)	25 mL
2	onions, chopped	2
8	cloves garlic, minced	8
½ tsp	ground cloves	2 mL
½ tsp	dried oregano leaves	2 mL
1	jar (26 oz/700 mL) Classico di Capri Sun-Dried Tomato Pasta Sauce	1
1 cup	dry red wine	250 mL
1 cup	beef stock or water	250 mL
2	bay leaves	2
10 oz	pearl onions, peeled (see Tip, page 121)	300 g

Variation

Substitute lamb for the pork.

1. Season pork with salt and pepper. In a large heavy saucepan, heat oil over medium-high heat. Add pork, in batches, and cook until all sides are browned. Remove and set aside.

2. Add more oil to pan, if required. Add onions and cook until softened, about 6 to 7 minutes. Add garlic, cloves and oregano. Cook for 2 to 3 minutes.

3. Add the reserved pork, pasta sauce, wine, stock and bay leaves. Bring to a boil. Reduce heat to low and simmer, covered, for 1½ hours. Add pearl onions and simmer for 30 minutes more. Remove bay leaves and serve.

Tip: If you prefer to bake your stew, place the stew in an ovenproof baking casserole. Cover and cook in a preheated 325°F (160°C) oven for the same amount of time as above.

Home-Style Beef Stew

Busy people are often looking for recipes that freeze well that they can cook when they have time, then freeze extra portions for another meal. Not only does this zesty stew meet that requirement, it is so good it will quickly become a favorite.

SERVE 4 TO 6

- PREHEAT OVEN TO 325°F (160°C)
- DUTCH OVEN
- 16-CUP (4 L) BAKING CASSEROLE WITH LID

2½ lbs	boneless beef shank, cut into 1½-inch (4 cm) cubes	1.25 kg
	Salt and freshly ground black pepper	
	All-purpose flour	
⅓ cup	vegetable oil, divided	75 mL
3	cloves garlic, minced	3
1	large onion, chopped	1
1½ cups	beef stock or water	375 mL
1	jar (26 oz/700 mL) Classico di Roma Arrabbiata Spicy Red Pepper Pasta Sauce	1
2	sprigs fresh thyme	2
2	bay leaves	2
3	carrots, chopped	3
2	new white potatoes, chopped	2
1 cup	frozen green peas, thawed	250 mL

Variation
Use boneless lean stew beef, if beef shank is not available.

1. Season beef with salt and pepper and lightly roll in flour to coat.

2. In a Dutch oven, heat 2 tbsp (25 mL) oil over medium-high heat. Add beef, in batches, and brown on all sides, adding more oil when required. Remove beef and reserve.

3. Add garlic and onion to the pan. Cook for 5 to 6 minutes. Add stock, pasta sauce, thyme and bay leaves. Bring to a boil.

continued on page 88

4. Place beef in casserole dish. Pour heated stock mixture over beef. Cover and bake in preheated oven for 1 hour. Add carrots and potatoes. Bake until the vegetables and beef are tender, about 1½ hours more. Stir in peas during the last 5 minutes of cooking. Adjust seasoning, if required.

....

Tip: This stew freezes well. Cool, portion and freeze for up to 2 months.

Other Great Recipes Featuring
Classico di Roma Arrabbiata
Spicy Red Pepper Pasta Sauce

Entertaining
Spicy Italian Seafood Stew (*page 176*)
Steamed Mussels in a Spicy Tomato Broth (*page 182*)

Pasta
Classic Vegetarian Lasagna (*page 66*)
Fettuccine with Shrimp and Mussels (*page 76*)

For a complete list of recipes using this sauce,
see Index by Sauce (*page 185*).

Pork Chops with Peppers

Here's an easy way to transform simple pork chops into a great meal. There's even a secret to keeping them juicy. Serve this wonderful dish over hot spaghetti.

4	pork chops, about 1 inch (2.5 cm) thick	4
	Salt and freshly ground black pepper	
	All-purpose flour	
2 tbsp	olive oil (approx.)	25 mL
2	cloves garlic, minced	2
1	green bell pepper, cut into strips	1
1	red bell pepper, cut into strips	1
1	onion, cut into wedges	1
1/3 cup	dry white wine, optional	75 mL
1	jar (26 oz/700 mL) Classico di Napoli Tomato & Basil Pasta Sauce	1
12 oz	spaghetti	375 g

Variation
Substitute pork chops with boneless skinless chicken breasts.

1. Season pork chops with salt and pepper and lightly toss in flour.

2. In a large saucepan, heat oil over medium-high heat. Add two pork chops at a time and brown on both sides. Remove pork chops and set aside.

3. Add more oil to saucepan, if required. Add garlic, peppers and onion. Cook until tender, about 6 to 7 minutes. Add wine, if using, and cook until wine has almost evaporated, about 1 to 2 minutes. Stir in pasta sauce and heat through.

4. Return pork chops to saucepan. (This is the secret to keeping them juicy.) Bring to a boil. Reduce heat and simmer, covered, until pork chops are cooked through and just a hint of pink remains, about 12 to 15 minutes.

5. Meanwhile, cook spaghetti according to package instructions. Serve pork chops and sauce over spaghetti.

Rice and Beef-Stuffed Peppers

Make this dish when local peppers are in season and enjoy a delicious meal with outstanding eye appeal. The peppers don't take long to assemble, then they are popped in the oven to bake. Just add some crusty bread and a tossed salad.

SERVES 6

- PREHEAT OVEN TO 350°F (180°C)
- 14-CUP (3.5 L) BAKING DISH

6	large red, green or yellow bell peppers	6
2 tbsp	olive oil	25 mL
1	onion, finely chopped	1
8 oz	mushrooms, finely chopped	250 g
¼ cup	finely chopped fresh parsley	50 mL
1 lb	lean ground beef	500 g
1 cup	cooked rice, about 6 tbsp (90 mL) dry	250 mL
⅓ cup	freshly grated Parmesan or Romano cheese	75 mL
¼ cup	dry bread crumbs	50 mL
1	jar (26 oz/700 mL) Classico di Firenze Florentine Spinach & Cheese Pasta Sauce	1
	Salt and freshly ground black pepper	
1	egg, beaten	1

Variation
Use veal or sausage in place of the beef.

1. Cut tops off peppers and set aside. Remove the seeds and membrane from each pepper.

2. In a saucepan, heat oil over medium heat. Add onion, mushrooms and parsley. Cook until tender, about 6 to 7 minutes. Remove from heat and cool.

3. In a large bowl, combine cooked onion-mushroom mixture with beef, rice, cheese, bread crumbs and ¼ cup (50 mL) pasta sauce. Season with salt and pepper. Mix in egg.

4. Spread remaining pasta sauce in baking dish. Fill peppers with beef mixture and replace tops. Place peppers in prepared baking dish. Bake, covered, in preheated oven until peppers are tender and meat has cooked through, about 1 hour. Serve peppers topped with sauce.

Braised Short Ribs

Short ribs are a particularly flavorful cut of beef and they respond well to a wide variety of seasonings. In this tasty braise, the ribs are slowly cooked in a vegetable and tomato sauce with a hint of vinegar. After the long, leisurely cooking, the meat becomes so tender that it falls off the bone. Delectable!

SERVES 4

- PREHEAT OVEN TO 325°F (160°C)
- 16-CUP (4 L) BAKING CASSEROLE WITH LID

4 lbs	short ribs, cut into 2½-inch (6 cm) pieces	2 kg
	Salt and freshly ground black pepper	
2 tbsp	olive oil (approx.)	25 mL
2 tbsp	butter (approx.)	25 mL
1	onion, diced	1
1	carrot, diced	1
1	stalk celery, diced	1
5	cloves garlic, minced	5
5 to 6	sprigs fresh thyme	5 to 6
2 tbsp	red wine vinegar	25 mL
1	jar (26 oz/700 mL) Classico di Napoli Tomato & Basil Pasta Sauce	1
1 cup	beef stock or water (approx.)	250 mL
	Fresh thyme sprigs	

1. Season ribs with salt and pepper. In a large deep saucepan, heat oil and butter over medium-high heat. Add ribs, in batches, and brown on all sides, adding more butter and oil as required. Remove and set aside.

2. Add onion, carrot, celery and garlic to saucepan. Cook until tender, about 6 to 7 minutes. Return ribs to saucepan. Add thyme, vinegar, pasta sauce and enough stock to come up the sides but not over the ribs. Bring to a boil. Remove from heat.

3. Transfer to casserole dish. Cover and bake in preheated oven until ribs are tender, about 2 to 2½ hours. Remove ribs. Skim off fat from sauce, if required. Cook sauce over medium heat until just thickened. Return ribs and heat through. Serve topped with thyme sprigs.

Tip: For sheer comfort food, serve this dish with creamy mashed potatoes.

Other Great Recipes Featuring
Classico di Napoli Tomato & Basil Pasta Sauce

Meat
Braised Veal Shank (*page 98*)
Pork Chops with Peppers (*page 89*)

Pasta
Penne with Tomato Cream Vodka Sauce (*page 56*)

For a complete list of recipes using this sauce,
see Index by Sauce (*page 185*).

Stuffed Pork Tenderloin with Mushrooms

This recipe is impressive enough to serve to guests. Lean pork tenderloin is stuffed with a filling of bacon, mushrooms, garlic, bread crumbs and basil pesto, then roasted (or grilled, if you prefer) until succulent. Simple, but delicious, this recipe is ideal for the buffet table as it can be served at room temperature.

SERVES 4 TO 6

• PREHEAT OVEN TO 375°F (190°C)

4	slices bacon, chopped	4
2 cups	chopped mushrooms, such as shiitake and button mushrooms, about 6 oz (175 g)	500 mL
2	cloves garlic, minced	2
Pinch	salt	Pinch
½ cup	fresh bread crumbs	125 mL
¼ cup	Classico di Genova Basil Pesto	50 mL
2	pork tenderloins, about 1½ lbs (750 g)	2

1. In a skillet over medium heat, cook bacon until golden and crisp. Transfer bacon to paper towel. Drain all but 1 tbsp (15 mL) fat from skillet.

2. Add mushrooms, garlic and salt. Cook over medium-high heat until golden brown, about 5 to 7 minutes. Transfer to a bowl. Stir in bacon, bread crumbs and 2 tbsp (25 mL) pesto until well combined.

3. Trim any fat from tenderloins. Using a sharp knife, cut in half lengthwise, almost, but not all the way through. Open out flat. Spoon stuffing evenly along center. Fold thin ends over filling, then fold sides shut to enclose. With a long wooden skewer, sew seam shut by threading through at 2-inch (5 cm) intervals, or tie with kitchen string. Spread remaining pesto over outside of tenderloins.

continued on page 96

4. Place tenderloins on rack in roasting pan. Roast in preheated oven until juices run clear when meat is pierced and just a hint of pink remains, about 30 to 35 minutes. Tent with foil and let stand for 10 minutes. Turn tenderloins over. With clean cloth, hold tenderloin firmly and pull out skewer. Cut into 1-inch (2.5 cm) slices. Serve with roast potatoes and sugar snap peas.

Tip: To grill tenderloins, place on greased grill over medium heat with lid closed, turning occasionally, until juices run clear when meat is pierced and just a hint of pink remains, about 35 minutes. Brush with pesto during the last 2 to 3 minutes of grilling time.

Tip: Tenderloins can be stuffed, wrapped tightly in plastic wrap and refrigerated for up to 6 hours. Spread pesto on outside of pork just before roasting.

Other Great Recipes Featuring
Classico di Genova Basil Pesto

Appetizer
White Bean Dip with Lemon (*page 20*)

Entertaining
Golden Cherry Tomato and Pesto Tart (*page 174*)
Pesto-Crusted Rack of Lamb with Feta (*page 170*)

Salad
Romaine and Radicchio Salad with Creamy Pesto Dressing (*page 33*)

Vegetarian
Genoa Pizza (*page 157*)

For a complete list of recipes using this sauce,
see Index by Sauce (*page 185*).

Sun-Dried Tomato Pesto and Cheese-Stuffed Pork Chops

Here's a great idea for a special meal as it requires a minimum of effort. Pork chops are filled with feta cheese, sun-dried tomato pesto and parsley, then browned and roasted until the cheese has melted, creating a delicious center. For a change, try making this recipe with boneless chicken breasts instead of the pork chops.

SERVES 4

Variation
Replace feta with goat cheese and parsley with basil.

• PREHEAT OVEN TO 400°F (200°C)
• OVENPROOF SKILLET

4	boneless pork loin chops, about ⅓ inch (2 cm) thick	4
⅓ cup	crumbled feta cheese	75 mL
3 tbsp	Classico di Sardegna Sun-Dried Tomato Pesto	45 mL
1 tbsp	finely chopped fresh parsley	15 mL
	Salt and freshly ground black pepper	
1 tbsp	olive oil	15 mL

1. Insert tip of sharp knife horizontally into long side of each pork chop. Cut almost, but not all the way through, to the other side, moving knife back and forth to form a pocket in the chop.

2. Combine feta cheese, pesto and parsley. Divide equally among pork chops, spooning into pockets and pressing lightly on top of chops to distribute evenly. Secure open side with small skewers or toothpicks. Sprinkle with salt and pepper.

3. In a skillet, heat oil over medium-high heat. Cook chops until golden brown on both sides. Transfer pan to preheated oven. Roast until cheese is melted and just a hint of pink remains, about 12 to 15 minutes. Remove skewers to serve.

Tip: To make a plastic or wooden skillet handle ovenproof, simply wrap in several layers of heavy-duty foil.

Braised Veal Shank

Here's an easy-to-make but mouth-watering version of the Italian classic Osso Buco. In this recipe, the veal shanks are slowly simmered in a vegetable and tomato sauce, enhanced with white wine and herbs. When cooked, the succulent meat just falls off the bone. Try to use flat-leaf or Italian parsley for flavor and authenticity and, to continue the Italian theme, accompany with a simple risotto.

SERVES 6

- PREHEAT OVEN TO 325°F (160°C)
- 16-CUP (4 L) BAKING CASSEROLE WITH A LID

6	veal shank pieces, each about 12 oz (375 g)	6
	Salt and freshly ground black pepper	
	All-purpose flour	
⅓ cup	olive oil, divided	75 mL
1½ cups	diced onion, about 3 medium	375 mL
1½ cups	diced carrot, about 3 medium	375 mL
1½ cups	diced celery, about 3 stalks	375 mL
4	cloves garlic, minced	4
1 cup	dry white wine	250 mL
1	jar (26 oz/700 mL) Classico di Napoli Tomato & Basil Pasta Sauce	1
3 cups	homemade or prepared veal or chicken stock	750 mL
¼ cup	chopped fresh parsley	50 mL

1. Season veal with salt and pepper and lightly toss in flour.

2. In a large saucepan, heat 3 tbsp (45 mL) oil. Brown veal shanks, in batches, on all sides. Remove and set aside. Wipe out pan, if required.

continued on page 100

3. Add remaining oil to saucepan. Heat over medium heat. Add onions, carrots, celery and garlic. Cook until just tender, about 6 to 7 minutes. Stir in wine and cook for 1 to 2 minutes. Add pasta sauce and stock. Bring to a boil. Remove from heat.

4. Place veal in casserole dish. Pour sauce over veal. Cover and bake in preheated oven for 2 hours or until the veal is tender. Transfer to serving platter and cover to keep warm. Simmer sauce until slightly reduced, if desired. Season with salt and pepper to taste. Stir in parsley. Spoon sauce over veal and serve.

Tip: This recipe holds well overnight. Make the day before and reheat in a warm oven.

Other Great Recipes Featuring
Classico di Napoli Tomato & Basil Pasta Sauce

Appetizer
Eggplant and Cheese Rolls (*page 17*)

Chicken
Tuscan Chicken with Garlic and Capers (*page 110*)

Fish
Mediterranean Fish Stew (*page 140*)

For a complete list of recipes using this sauce,
see Index by Sauce (*page 185*).

Pork Tenderloin with Cream Sauce

This delicious dish is elegant enough to serve to company and it takes only 20 minutes to prepare! Serve with tiny roasted potatoes and a tangy salad of baby greens for a great-tasting meal.

SERVES 6

2	pork tenderloins, about 1½ lbs (750 g)	2
Pinch	salt	Pinch
2 tbsp	butter	25 mL
1	leek, white and light green part only, washed and chopped (see Tip, page 28)	1
½ cup	dry white wine	125 mL
1½ cups	whipping (35%) cream	375 mL
2 tbsp	Classico di Sardegna Sun-Dried Tomato Pesto	25 mL

1. Cut pork into ½-inch (1 cm) slices and season with salt. In a skillet, melt butter over medium-high heat. Cook pork, in batches, until golden brown, about 2 minutes per side. Transfer to plate and keep warm.

2. Reduce heat to medium. Cook leek until softened, about 3 to 5 minutes. Add wine and cook until reduced by half.

3. Add cream and bring to boil. Simmer until thick enough to coat the back of a spoon, about 3 to 5 minutes. Stir in pesto. Return pork to pan for 1 minute, turning to coat and warm through. Serve at once.

Variations

Replace pork tenderloin with chicken breasts or veal chops.

Add ½ cup (125 mL) diced red pepper and ½ tsp (2 mL) grated lemon zest.

Roast Leg of Lamb with Tomato, Artichoke and Peppers

A simple leg of lamb takes on new dimensions when touched with the flavors of the sunny Mediterranean. This recipe combines the wonderful flavors of olive oil, lemon and oregano with a traditionally Italian finish of artichokes and peppers in a tomato and roasted garlic sauce.

SERVES 8

• PREHEAT OVEN TO 350°F (180°C)

3 lbs	boneless leg of lamb	1.5 kg
4	cloves garlic, minced	4
¼ cup	olive oil	50 mL
⅓ cup	chopped fresh oregano, divided	75 mL
1 tbsp	grated lemon zest	15 mL
2 tbsp	lemon juice	25 mL
¼ tsp	salt	1 mL
1	can (14 oz/398 mL) artichokes, drained and cut into quarters	1
1	each small green and red bell pepper, seeded and sliced	1
1	jar (26 oz/700 mL) Classico di Sorrento Roasted Garlic Pasta Sauce	1

1. Place lamb in glass or ceramic dish. Combine garlic, oil, ¼ cup (50 mL) oregano, lemon zest, juice and salt. Pour over lamb, turning to coat. Cover and refrigerate for 2 hours.

2. Transfer lamb to roasting pan. Discard any leftover marinade. Roast in preheated oven for 1 hour.

3. Drain any fat from pan. Add remaining oregano, artichokes and peppers. Pour sauce over vegetables. Return to oven and roast until meat thermometer reads 150°F (70°C) for medium-rare, about 30 to 40 minutes more or to desired doneness. Remove from oven. Tent with foil and let stand for 10 minutes. Transfer lamb to serving platter. Slice thinly and serve with sauce and vegetables.

....

Tip: If you don't have fresh oregano, replace with 3 tbsp (45 mL) chopped fresh parsley and 4 tsp (20 mL) dried oregano.

Tip: Some boneless leg of lamb comes wrapped in stretchable netting. Remove the netting and tie leg at 1-inch (2.5 cm) intervals with kitchen string.

Siena Lamb Chops

Here's a dynamite recipe for lamb chops, inspired by the Italian countryside. The succulent chops are marinated in a lively vinaigrette enhanced with Dijon mustard and garden-fresh herbs. After being grilled or broiled, they are served on top of a zesty roasted tomato and vegetable sauce. Add some couscous or a simple risotto to complete the meal.

SERVES 4

• PREHEAT BROILER OR PREHEAT BARBECUE TO MEDIUM HEAT

¼ cup	red wine vinegar	50 mL
2 tbsp	olive oil	25 mL
2 tbsp	chopped fresh thyme or 2 tsp (10 mL) dried	25 mL
2 tbsp	chopped fresh basil leaves or 2 tsp (10 mL) dried	25 mL
2 tsp	chopped fresh rosemary or ½ tsp (2 mL) dried	10 mL
1 tsp	Dijon mustard	5 mL
¼ tsp	salt	1 mL
¼ tsp	freshly ground black pepper	1 mL
12	lamb loin chops, about 2½ lbs (1.25 kg)	12
½	batch Fire-Roasted Sauce (see recipe, page 106)	½

1. In a glass dish, whisk together vinegar, oil, thyme, basil, rosemary, Dijon, salt and pepper. Add lamb chops, turning to coat. Marinate for 15 minutes at room temperature or refrigerate for up to 6 hours.

2. Broil chops, turning once, until desired doneness, about 6 minutes per side for medium-rare. Alternately, cook on greased preheated grill until desired doneness, about 7 minutes per side for medium-rare.

3. Spread Fire-Roasted Sauce on a serving platter and arrange chops over top.

Fire-Roasted Sauce

This sauce was inspired by the town of Siena, where homemade recipes often combine roasted tomatoes with garlic for a robust sauce.

MAKES 5 CUPS
(1.25 L)

1 tbsp	olive oil	15 mL
1	onion, chopped	1
1	zucchini, chopped	1
½	green bell pepper, seeded and chopped	½
1	jar (26 oz/700 mL) Classico di Siena Fire-Roasted Tomato & Garlic Pasta Sauce	1
½ cup	water	125 mL
½ cup	chopped black olives	125 mL

1. In a skillet, heat oil over medium-high heat. Cook onion, zucchini and green pepper until tender, about 3 to 5 minutes. Add pasta sauce, water and olives. Bring to boil. Reduce heat and simmer for 15 minutes.

Tip: This sauce is good with pasta, chicken or over a mushroom omelet. Store sauce covered in the refrigerator for 2 to 3 days or freeze in plastic containers for up to 2 months.

Easy Pot Roast

There's nothing quite like pot roast for a family Sunday dinner. The wonderful aromas that drift through the house as it cooks are characteristically hearth and home. With this recipe, the meal practically cooks itself — just turn the roast once, add the vegetables and thicken the gravy at the last minute.

SERVES 6 TO 8

Variation
Replace wine with beef stock.

• PREHEAT OVEN TO 350°F (180°C)
• LARGE DEEP SAUCEPAN OR DUTCH OVEN WITH LID

⅓ cup	all-purpose flour	150 mL
4 lbs	cross rib, blade or rump roast	2 kg
2 tbsp	vegetable oil	25 mL
½ cup	dry red wine	125 mL
1	jar (26 oz/700 mL) Classico di Toscana Portobello Mushroom Pasta Sauce	1
½ cup	beef stock	125 mL
6	carrots, halved crosswise	6
4	new white potatoes, quartered	4
4	small onions, halved	4
1 tsp	granulated sugar	5 mL

1. Spread flour on a plate. Pat roast dry and roll in flour to coat, reserving any excess. In a saucepan, heat oil over medium-high heat. Brown roast all over. Add wine. Bring to boil and reduce for 2 minutes. Add pasta sauce and beef stock. Cover and cook in preheated oven for 2½ hours.

2. Turn roast over. Add carrots, potatoes and onions to pan. Cover and cook until vegetables are tender, about 45 to 60 minutes.

3. Remove roast and vegetables from pan. Keep warm. Whisk reserved flour with ¼ cup (50 mL) cold water, then whisk in about ½ cup (125 mL) hot liquid from pan. Whisk mixture back into pan along with sugar. Bring to a boil over high heat and cook, stirring until thickened, about 3 to 5 minutes. Slice roast thinly. Serve with sauce and vegetables.

Tip: Use tongs or wooden spoons to turn the roast. Piercing it lets the juices flow out during cooking, making the meat less moist.

Chicken

~

Tuscan Chicken with Garlic and Capers

Tuscan Chicken with Garlic and Capers

On their own, the strong flavor of anchovies can be overpowering, but used with discretion they bring out the best in many ingredients, particularly tomatoes. Try this easy dish when your taste buds need a pick-me-up. It's equally delicious over fluffy mashed potatoes or steamed white rice.

SERVES 4

4	boneless, skinless chicken breasts, pounded to ½-inch (1 cm) thickness	4
	Salt and freshly ground black pepper	
	All-purpose flour	
¼ cup	olive oil	50 mL
2	cloves garlic, minced	2
1	onion, finely chopped	1
½ cup	dry white wine	125 mL
2 tbsp	capers	25 mL
2	anchovy fillets, finely chopped, optional	2
1	jar (26 oz/700 mL) Classico di Napoli Tomato & Basil Pasta Sauce	1
	Chopped fresh parsley, basil or oregano	

Variation
Stir a few pitted olives into the sauce for a nice flavor change.

1. Season chicken with salt and pepper and lightly toss in flour.

2. In a large saucepan, heat oil over medium-high heat. Add chicken and cook until golden and no longer pink inside, about 2 to 3 minutes per side. Remove chicken and set aside.

3. Add garlic and onion to saucepan. Cook until softened, about 6 to 7 minutes. Stir in wine and cook until the wine has nearly evaporated. Add capers, anchovy fillets, if using, and pasta sauce. Simmer for 3 to 4 minutes. Return chicken to saucepan and heat through. Serve chicken topped with sauce and parsley.

Tip: Ask the butcher to pound out the chicken to save you a step.

Chicken Gumbo

Gumbo is a classic stew-like dish. One hallmark of a true gumbo is a roux — oil and flour cooked together until golden. Another is okra, a green pod-like vegetable with a taste reminiscent of eggplant that is also used to thicken the dish. Add a medley of other ingredients and you have this delicious meal in a bowl. Serve with warm crusty bread for a down-home treat.

SERVES 4 TO 6

1½ lbs	boneless, skinless chicken thighs	750 g
4 oz	Black Forest ham in one thick slice	125 g
2 tbsp	vegetable oil	25 mL
2 tbsp	all-purpose flour	25 mL
1 cup	chopped onion, about 2 medium	250 mL
1 cup	chopped celery, about 2 stalks	250 mL
1 cup	chopped green bell pepper, about 1 medium	250 mL
1 tsp	dried thyme leaves	5 mL
¼ tsp	cayenne pepper, (or to taste)	1 mL
1	bay leaf	1
1	jar (26 oz/700 mL) Classico di Piemonte Red Wine & Herb Pasta Sauce	1
1¾ cups	water	425 mL
1 cup	sliced frozen okra, about 16, thawed	250 mL

Variation
Replace okra with 1 cup (250 mL) frozen green peas.

1. Cut chicken into 1½-inch (4 cm) pieces. Cut ham into ½-inch (1 cm) pieces. Set aside.

2. In a large saucepan, whisk together oil and flour over medium heat. Cook, stirring constantly, until a butterscotch color, about 3 to 5 minutes. Add ham, onions, celery, green pepper, thyme and cayenne. Cook, stirring, for 3 minutes.

3. Add chicken, bay leaf, pasta sauce and water. Bring to a boil, reduce heat and simmer, uncovered, until chicken is tender, about 25 to 30 minutes. Add okra and simmer for 5 minutes. Remove bay leaf and serve.

Tip: Frozen whole okra is easiest to slice when still partially frozen.

Chicken and Asparagus Toss

An Italian take on stir-fries that's ready in 15 minutes is sure to please. Serve with noodles, rice or polenta.

1 lb	asparagus	500 g
2 tbsp	olive oil, divided	25 mL
1 lb	boneless, skinless chicken breasts, thinly sliced	500 g
1	red bell pepper, cored and thinly sliced	1
1	yellow bell pepper, cored and thinly sliced	1
1	red onion, cut into thin wedges	1
½ cup	Classico di Genova Basil Pesto	125 mL
½ cup	chicken stock	125 mL
1 tsp	cornstarch	5 mL

1. Trim woody ends from asparagus. Cut into 2-inch (5 cm) pieces. Set aside.

2. In a wok or large skillet, heat 1 tbsp (15 mL) oil over high heat. Stir-fry chicken, in batches, until golden. Transfer to a plate.

3. Add remaining oil to wok. Stir-fry red pepper, yellow pepper, onion and asparagus until tender-crisp, about 3 to 4 minutes.

4. Meanwhile, whisk together pesto, chicken stock and cornstarch. Add to wok, stirring until thickened. Toss with chicken and serve at once.

Tip: When buying asparagus, look for firm, green-colored stalks with tightly closed tips.

Variation

Replace Classico di Genova Basil Pesto with 1 jar (26 oz/700 mL) Classico di Napoli Tomato & Basil Pasta Sauce. In a large skillet, stir in pasta sauce after vegetables have cooked and reduce heat to medium-low. Simmer, stirring occasionally, about 4 to 5 minutes. Season with salt and pepper to taste. Omit chicken stock and cornstarch. Toss with chicken and serve.

Braised Chicken with Eggplant

Here's a dish that captures the robust flavors of Mediterranean cooking, yet it's easy enough to make during a weeknight. Serve this savory stew with plenty of crusty bread to soak up the rich, flavorful sauce.

SERVES 4

• LARGE DUTCH OVEN WITH COVER

1	leek, white and light green part only (see Tip, page 28)	1
½ cup	pitted green olives	125 mL
4	bone-in, skinless chicken breasts	4
	All-purpose flour	
⅓ cup	olive oil, divided	75 mL
2	cloves garlic, minced	2
½ cup	chicken stock	125 mL
1	jar (26 oz/700 mL) Classico di Piemonte Red Wine & Herb Pasta Sauce	1
1	eggplant	1

1. Cut leek in half lengthwise. Slice thinly and rinse under cold running water. Set aside to drain. Cut olives in quarters. Set aside.

2. Coat chicken lightly with flour. Heat 2 tbsp (25 mL) oil in Dutch oven. Brown chicken on both sides. Transfer to a plate. Add leek and garlic to Dutch oven. Cook over medium heat until tender. Stir in stock and olives, scraping up any brown bits from bottom of pan. Stir in pasta sauce.

3. Nestle chicken in sauce. Bring to a boil. Reduce heat to medium-low, cover and simmer, turning chicken once, until chicken is no longer pink inside, about 20 to 25 minutes.

4. Meanwhile, peel eggplant and cut into 1-inch (2.5 cm) pieces. In a skillet, heat remaining oil over medium-high heat. Add eggplant and cook, stirring often, until browned. Remove and set aside. Add eggplant to Dutch oven. Simmer, uncovered, until heated through, about 2 to 3 minutes.

Variations

Substitute 8 bone-in, skinless chicken thighs for breasts.

For chicken with eggplant puttanesca-style, add 1 tbsp (15 mL) capers and ½ tsp (2 mL) hot pepper flakes with olives.

Chicken Enchiladas

This tasty dish is certain to be requested often. Chicken, cheese and spinach are nestled in a flour tortilla and baked in a spicy tomato sauce. Serve this with a simple salad of Boston lettuce, green onions and chopped avocado in an oil and vinegar dressing for a great meal.

SERVES 6

Variation
Replace chicken with 1 lb (500 g) lean beef steak.

- PREHEAT OVEN TO 350°F (180°C)
- 13-BY 9-INCH (3 L) BAKING PAN

2 tbsp	olive oil	25 mL
2	boneless, skinless chicken breasts	2
4	green onions, thinly sliced	4
4 oz	baby spinach	125 g
1/4 tsp	dried oregano leaves	1 mL
Pinch	cayenne pepper	Pinch
2 cups	shredded Monterey Jack or Cheddar cheese	500 mL
	Salt and freshly ground black pepper	
1	jar (26 oz/700 mL) Classico di Roma Arrabbiata Spicy Red Pepper Pasta Sauce	1
6	large 10-inch (25 cm) soft flour tortillas	6

1. In a large saucepan, heat oil over medium heat. Add chicken breasts and cook until golden and no longer pink inside, about 5 to 6 minutes per side. Remove, cool and cut into bite-size pieces.

2. Add green onions, spinach, oregano and cayenne pepper to saucepan. Cook until spinach begins to wilt, about 1 to 2 minutes. Remove from heat. Stir into spinach mixture 1/4 cup (50 mL) pasta sauce, reserved chicken and 1 cup (250 mL) cheese. Mix well. Season with salt and pepper to taste.

3. Spread 1 cup (250 mL) sauce in bottom of baking pan. Place about 1/2 cup (125 mL) chicken mixture on each tortilla, roll up and transfer to baking pan seam-side down. Pour remaining sauce evenly over filled tortillas. Bake, uncovered, in preheated oven until hot and bubbly, about 25 to 30 minutes. Sprinkle with remaining cheese and bake until cheese melts, about 5 minutes more.

Ham and Cheese- Stuffed Chicken Rolls

Here's a simplified version of Chicken Cordon Bleu that is every bit as delicious as the original. This dish works equally well as the centerpiece of a casual supper or an elegant dinner. Add potatoes, sprinkled with parsley, and steamed asparagus and wait for the compliments.

SERVES 6

- PREHEAT OVEN TO 375°F (190°C)
- 13-BY 9-INCH (3 L) BAKING PAN

2 tbsp	butter	25 mL
1	onion, finely chopped	1
8 oz	assorted mushrooms, finely chopped	250 g
¼ cup	dry bread crumbs	50 mL
¼ cup	freshly grated Romano cheese	50 mL
2 tbsp	pine nuts, optional	25 mL
2 tbsp	chopped fresh parsley	25 mL
	Salt and freshly ground black pepper	
1	egg, beaten	1
6	thin slices smoked ham	6
6	boneless, skinless chicken breasts, pounded to ¼-inch (0.5 cm) thickness	6
1	jar (26 oz/700 mL) Classico di Piemonte Red Wine & Herb Pasta Sauce	1

Variation

Use thinly sliced prosciutto in place of smoked ham.

1. In a skillet, melt butter over medium heat. Add onion and mushrooms. Cook until tender, about 6 to 7 minutes. Remove from heat and cool. Mix in bread crumbs, cheese, pine nuts, if using, and parsley. Season with salt and pepper to taste. Mix in egg.

2. Lay one piece of ham over each chicken breast. Divide mushroom mixture evenly among each ham-topped chicken breast. Roll up each piece and tie with butcher's twine.

3. Pour half the sauce in bottom of baking pan. Place each chicken roll in pan and cover with remaining sauce.

4. Bake, uncovered, in preheated oven until chicken is no longer pink inside, about 30 minutes. To serve, snip string off and top each chicken bundle with sauce.

Chicken with Green Olives

The bold flavors in this recipe are the perfect antidote to a chilly day. Ladle over buttermilk mashed potatoes for a comfort food treat.

SERVES 4

- PREHEAT OVEN TO 375°F (190°C)
- OVENPROOF SAUCEPAN

2 tbsp	olive oil, divided	25 mL
4	bone-in, skinless chicken breasts	4
2	large carrots, peeled and thinly sliced	2
2	stalks celery, sliced	2
1	onion, sliced into 8 wedges	1
¾ cup	diced ham, about 3 oz (90 g)	175 mL
½ cup	halved, pitted green olives	125 mL
1	jar (26 oz/700 mL) Classico di Genoa Tomato & Pesto Pasta Sauce	1

1. In a large ovenproof saucepan, heat 1 tbsp (15 mL) oil over medium-high heat. Cook chicken breasts until golden brown on both sides. Transfer to a plate.

2. Reduce heat to medium. Add remaining oil to saucepan. Add carrots, celery, onion and ham. Cook until tender, about 5 to 7 minutes. Stir in green olives and sauce. Nestle chicken breasts into sauce.

3. Bring to a boil. Cover and bake in preheated oven until chicken breasts are no longer pink inside, about 30 to 35 minutes. Remove chicken and tent with foil to keep warm. Remove saucepan with sauce from oven and simmer on stovetop until nicely thickened. Serve over chicken.

Tip: For diced ham, ask the deli counter to give you several slices ¼ inch (1 cm) thick.

Tip: To make buttermilk mashed potatoes: Boil 2 lbs (1 kg) peeled potatoes in salted boiling water until fork-tender. Drain well. Mash in pot with 1 cup (250 mL) buttermilk, 2 tbsp (25 mL) butter and ½ tsp (2 mL) each salt and pepper. For an added flavor option, stir in 2 minced green onions and 2 tbsp (25 mL) chopped fresh parsley, if desired.

Chicken Meatballs

These chicken meatballs, delicately seasoned with oregano and cumin and cooked in a flavorful sauce, are great family fare. This is also a good dish to have on hand for those hectic weeknights when everyone is coming and going. You can make the recipe ahead and keep it frozen until needed. Thaw, reheat and serve over hot pasta, couscous or polenta.

SERVES 4

1	egg, beaten	1
1/3 cup	grated onion, about 1/2 a medium onion	75 mL
1/4 cup	dry bread crumbs	50 mL
2 tbsp	finely chopped fresh parsley	25 mL
1 tsp	dried oregano leaves	5 mL
1 tsp	paprika	5 mL
1/2 tsp	salt	2 mL
1/2 tsp	ground cumin	2 mL
1 lb	ground chicken	500 g
2 tbsp	vegetable oil	25 mL
1	jar (26 oz/700 mL) Classico di Firenze Florentine Spinach & Cheese Pasta Sauce	1
1/2 cup	water	50 mL

Variation
Omit parsley, oregano, paprika and cumin. Add 2 tbsp (25 mL) Classico di Genova Basil Pesto with bread crumbs.

1. In a large bowl, stir egg with onion, bread crumbs, parsley, oregano, paprika, salt and cumin. Mix in chicken. Form into 1-inch (2.5 cm) balls.

2. In a skillet, heat oil over medium-high heat. Add meatballs and cook, turning often, until browned all over. Add pasta sauce and water. Simmer until meatballs are no longer pink inside, about 8 to 10 minutes.

Tip: Meatballs and sauce can be frozen in an airtight container for up to 1 month. Thaw in the refrigerator. To reheat, stir in an additional 1/4 cup (50 mL) water and simmer for 8 minutes.

Chicken with Mushrooms and Sun-Dried Tomato

Nothing could be easier than this superb one-pot recipe. Chicken pieces are browned, then simmered with mushrooms, garlic and pearl onions in white wine and a sun-dried tomato sauce. Add a crusty loaf and a simple salad for a delicious meal.

SERVES 6

• DUTCH OVEN OR LARGE SAUCEPAN

12	chicken pieces (see Tip, below)	12
	Salt and freshly ground black pepper	
	All-purpose flour	
3 tbsp	olive oil (approx.)	45 mL
1 lb	brown or white mushrooms, quartered	500 g
3	cloves garlic, minced	3
10 oz	pearl onions, peeled (see Tip, below)	300 g
½ cup	dry white wine	125 mL
1	jar (26 oz/700 mL) Classico di Capri Sun-Dried Tomato Pasta Sauce	1
	Chopped fresh parsley or basil leaves	

1. Season chicken with salt and pepper and lightly toss in flour.

2. In a Dutch oven or large saucepan, heat oil over medium-high heat. Add chicken, in batches, and brown on all sides, adding more oil, if required. Remove chicken and set aside.

3. Add mushrooms to Dutch oven and cook until tender. Add garlic and pearl onions. Cook for 1 to 2 minutes more. Stir in wine and cook until nearly evaporated. Stir in pasta sauce and heat through. Return chicken to Dutch oven. Cover and simmer until chicken is no longer pink inside, about 20 to 25 minutes. Serve chicken topped with sauce and parsley.

Tip: Chicken thighs and legs work the best in braised dishes because they stay moist.

Tip: To peel pearl onions: Place whole unpeeled onions in boiling water for 2 to 3 minutes. Drain the onions and rinse in cold water to cool. Cut off the tiny root ends and gently peel off the outermost layers of the onion.

Chicken Paella

Paella is a traditional rice dish that often contains abundant quantities of fresh seafood. This version, which can be made from ingredients that are readily available, is perfect for family dinners or casual dining with friends.

SERVES 4 TO 6

1 tbsp	olive oil (approx.)	15 mL
2	chorizo or mild Italian sausages	2
2	boneless, skinless chicken breasts, chopped	2
3	cloves garlic, minced	3
1	onion, chopped	1
1	yellow or green bell pepper, cut into strips	1
	Salt and freshly ground black pepper	
1½ cups	long-grain rice	375 mL
1¾ cups	chicken stock or water	425 mL
1	jar (26 oz/700 mL) Classico Italian Sausage, Peppers & Onions Pasta Sauce	1
1	can (14 oz/398 mL) artichoke hearts, drained and cut into quarters	1
1 cup	frozen green peas, thawed	250 mL

Variation

Try adding sautéed shrimp for another great taste.

1. In a large saucepan, heat oil over medium-high heat. Add sausages and cook until browned and juices run clear. Remove and set aside. Cool and slice into rounds.

2. Add chicken to saucepan and cook until on longer pink inside. Remove and set aside. Add garlic, onion and yellow pepper. Cook, stirring occasionally, until vegetables are tender, adding more oil, if required. Season with salt and pepper to taste. Add rice and cook for 1 to 2 minutes. Stir in stock and pasta sauce. Bring to a boil, reduce heat and simmer, covered, until rice is just tender, about 35 to 40 minutes.

3. Stir in sausage, chicken pieces, artichoke hearts and peas. Cover and continue to simmer until heated through, about 5 to 6 minutes. Adjust seasoning, if desired.

Four-Mushroom Chicken

Today, many varieties of mushrooms that would have been considered exotic years ago, have become commonplace in supermarkets. This delicious dish combines traditional button mushrooms with cremini and oyster mushrooms in a flavorful portobello mushroom sauce. Finished with cream, this recipe will do more than thrill your guests — it will have you in and out of the kitchen quickly so you can enjoy their company.

SERVES 6

2 tbsp	butter, divided	25 mL
2 tbsp	vegetable oil, divided	25 mL
6	boneless, skinless chicken breasts	6
2 cups	sliced button mushrooms, about 6 oz (175 g)	500 mL
2 cups	stemmed and sliced oyster mushrooms, about 6 oz (175 g)	500 mL
2 cups	sliced cremini mushrooms, about 6 oz (175 g)	500 mL
3	shallots, finely chopped	3
¼ tsp	salt	1 mL
¼ tsp	freshly ground black pepper	1 mL
½ cup	white wine	125 mL
2 tbsp	chopped fresh thyme leaves or 1½ tsp (7 mL) dried thyme leaves	25 mL
1	jar (26 oz/700 mL) Classico di Toscana Portobello Mushroom Pasta Sauce	1
⅓ cup	whipping (35%) cream	75 mL

1. In a large deep saucepan or Dutch oven, heat 1 tbsp (15 mL) each oil and butter over medium-high heat. Cook chicken breasts until golden brown on both sides. Transfer to a plate.

2. Add remaining butter and oil to skillet. Add button, oyster and cremini mushrooms, shallots, salt and pepper. Cook until browned and tender, about 4 to 6 minutes. Stir in wine and thyme. Cook until wine is nearly evaporated.

3. Return chicken to saucepan. Pour pasta sauce over top. Bring to a boil, reduce heat and simmer until chicken is no longer pink inside, about 10 minutes. Transfer chicken to a serving platter and cover with foil to keep warm. Stir cream into sauce. Bring to a boil. Remove from heat at once. Serve sauce over chicken.

Tip: Store mushrooms in a paper bag in the refrigerator. Rinse thoroughly under cold running water before trimming and slicing. Use at once.

Tip: For an attractive presentation, serve with buttered broad noodles, sprinkled with parsley.

Other Great Recipes Featuring
Classico di Toscana
Portobello Mushroom Pasta Sauce

Meat
Easy Pot Roast (*page 107*)

Pasta
Spaghettini Primavera (*page 49*)

Vegetarian
Baked Stuffed Zucchini (*page 162*)

For a complete list of recipes using this sauce,
see Index by Sauce (*page 185*).

Chicken Burgers

This is a great-tasting burger and here's the secret — a double hit of sun-dried tomato pesto — in the burger and slathered on the bun. All you need to add is a tossed salad for a delicious warm-weather meal.

SERVES 4

Variation
For more pesto flavor, try adding a small dollop on top of the burger as well as on the bun.

• INDOOR GRILL OR OUTDOOR BARBECUE, PREHEATED AND GREASED

1	egg	1
¼ cup	Classico di Sardegna Sun-Dried Tomato Pesto	50 mL
¼ tsp	salt	1 mL
¼ tsp	freshly ground black pepper	1 mL
1 lb	ground chicken or turkey	500 g
½ cup	dry bread crumbs	125 mL
2 tbsp	freshly grated Parmesan cheese	25 mL
2 oz	soft goat cheese	60 g
4	burger buns	4
2 tbsp	Classico di Sardegna Sun-Dried Tomato Pesto	25 mL
	Leaf lettuce	

1. In a large bowl, whisk together egg, pesto, salt and pepper. Add ground chicken, bread crumbs and Parmesan. Mix well. Form into 4 patties.

2. Place burgers on greased, preheated medium-hot grill. Close lid and cook for 5 minutes. Turn burgers and divide goat cheese evenly on top of each. Cook until meat is no longer pink inside, about 4 to 5 minutes.

3. Meanwhile, toast buns lightly on grill. Spread bottom of each bun with pesto. Top with lettuce, burger and top of bun.

Tip: You can also cook the burgers with 1 tbsp (15 mL) oil in a skillet over medium heat.

Tip: Burger patties can be made ahead and refrigerated for up to 4 hours or frozen for up to 1 week.

Cheese-Crusted Chicken Breasts

This almost effortless dish makes a great weeknight meal. Serve with linguine and steamed green beans.

SERVES 6

- PREHEAT OVEN TO 400°F (200°C)
- 13-BY 9-INCH (3 L) BAKING DISH

⅓ cup	dry bread crumbs	75 mL
⅓ cup	freshly grated Parmesan cheese	75 mL
1 tbsp	finely chopped fresh parsley	15 mL
¾ tsp	paprika	4 mL
6	boneless, skinless chicken breasts	6
1	egg, beaten	1
2 tbsp	olive oil (approx.)	25 mL
1	jar (26 oz/700 mL) Classico di Parma Four Cheese Pasta Sauce	1
¼ cup	water	50 mL
½ cup	grated Cheddar or Monterey Jack cheese	125 mL

1. In a shallow dish, combine bread crumbs, Parmesan, parsley and paprika. Dip chicken breasts in egg, then in bread crumb mixture, patting to adhere all over.

2. In a skillet, heat oil over medium-high heat. Cook chicken breasts until golden brown on both sides, adding more oil as needed. Transfer to a plate.

3. Pour sauce and water into baking dish. Place chicken on top. Bake in preheated oven for 20 minutes. Sprinkle chicken breasts with Cheddar. Bake until chicken is no longer pink inside and cheese is melted, about 5 minutes more.

Tip: Look for freshly grated Parmesan in the deli or cheese section of your supermarket. Store grated Parmesan in an airtight container in the freezer. Or buy a chunk of Parmesan and keep refrigerated, wrapped tightly in foil, and grate as needed.

Chicken Sauté with Sun-Dried Tomatoes

If you're really in a rush, try this speedy recipe. The sun-dried tomatoes add loads of flavor and flair to this tasty dish, which is ready in less than 15 minutes.

SERVES 6

6	boneless, skinless chicken breasts	6
3 tbsp	butter	45 mL
3 to 4	dry-packed sun-dried tomatoes, softened and finely chopped (see Tip, below)	3 to 4
3	green onions, finely chopped	3
1	jar (16 oz/435 mL) Classico Alfredo di Sorrento Roasted Garlic Pasta Sauce	1

1. Pound chicken to about $1/2$ inch (1 cm) thick.

2. In a large saucepan, melt butter over medium-high heat. Add chicken and cook on both sides until golden brown. Add sun-dried tomatoes and green onions. Cook for 1 minute more. Stir in pasta sauce and simmer (do not boil) until chicken is no longer pink inside, about 2 to 3 minutes. Serve immediately.

Tip: To soften sun-dried tomatoes, place in a bowl and cover with very hot water. Let stand for 2 to 3 minutes. Drain and pat dry.

Chicken with Capers and Roasted Peppers

Here's a no-fuss chicken sauté that couldn't be easier to make. The robust flavors of the capers and roasted red pepper mellow in the creamy Alfredo sauce.

SERVES 6

6	boneless, skinless chicken breasts	6
3 tbsp	butter	45 mL
½ cup	diced roasted red bell pepper, about 1 small (see Tip, page 70)	125 mL
2 tbsp	finely chopped fresh parsley (or to taste)	25 mL
1 tbsp	capers	15 mL
1	jar (16 oz/435 mL) Classico Alfredo di Roma Pasta Sauce	1

1. Pound chicken to about ½ inch (1 cm) thick.

2. In a large saucepan, melt butter over medium-high heat. Add chicken and cook on both sides until golden brown. Add roasted pepper, parsley, capers and pasta sauce. Simmer (do not boil) until chicken is no longer pink inside, about 2 to 3 minutes.

Tip: Complete this dish with delicious Tomato-Roasted Potatoes (see recipe, page 152) and a handful of cooked sugar snap peas.

Variation

Substitute 6 veal cutlets, about ¼ inch (0.5 cm) thick, for the chicken. Cook only 30 seconds per side, then add ingredients and simmer.

Fish and Seafood

∼

Pesto-Topped Salmon Kebobs

Pesto-Topped Salmon Kebobs

In this recipe, salmon is briefly steeped in a marinade for added flavor, then cooked on skewers for a dynamic presentation. A final brushing with basil pesto adds extra zest. To extend the dish, while adding color and pizzazz, thread multicolored peppers, cherry tomatoes and lemon wedges with the salmon. This is a great dish for a summer barbecue.

SERVES 4

- INDOOR GRILL OR OUTDOOR BARBECUE
- FOUR SKEWERS

2 lbs	salmon fillet, skin removed	1 kg
1½ tsp	Dijon mustard	7 mL
5 tbsp	lemon juice (or to taste)	75 mL
5 tbsp	olive oil	75 mL
	Salt and freshly ground black pepper	
6 tbsp	Classico di Genova Basil Pesto	90 mL

1. Cut salmon into sixteen 2-inch (5 cm) cubes. Thread salmon equally onto four skewers. Arrange kebobs in a single layer in a shallow glass dish.

2. Whisk together mustard, lemon juice and olive oil. Season with salt and pepper to taste. Pour over salmon kebobs. Cover and marinade at room temperature for 30 minutes.

3. Place kebobs on greased grill over medium heat. Cook, turning once, until fish is just cooked through, about 8 minutes. Brush each kebob with 1½ tbsp (22 mL) pesto and cook for 1 to 2 minutes more.

Tip: If you prefer, you can cook this dish in the oven. Remove fish from marinade and place in a baking dish. Bake in preheated 400°F (200°C) oven until fish is just cooked through, about 8 minutes. Remove and brush with pesto. Bake for 1 to 2 minutes more. Serve with steamed rice and your favorite vegetable.

Sea Bass with Tomato Pesto

Dinner will be ready before you know it with this delicious bake that is effortless to make. Simply prepare the sauce, then top with the fish and bake.

SERVES 6

Variation
Halibut and swordfish are good choices, too.

- PREHEAT OVEN TO 400°F (200°C)
- 13-BY 9-INCH (3 L) BAKING DISH

2 tbsp	olive oil	25 mL
2	cloves garlic, minced	2
1	onion, finely chopped	1
½ cup	dry white wine	125 mL
1	jar (26 oz/700 mL) Classico di Genoa Tomato & Pesto Pasta Sauce	1
¼ cup	chopped fresh basil or parsley	50 mL
6	sea bass fillets, each about 6 oz (175 g)	6
	Salt and freshly ground black pepper	

1. In a skillet, heat oil over medium heat. Add garlic and onion. Cook until softened, about 6 to 7 minutes. Add wine and cook for 1 to 2 minutes or until most of the wine has evaporated. Add pasta sauce and basil. Cook until sauce is heated through, about 2 to 3 minutes.

2. Spoon sauce into baking dish. Arrange fish over top. Sprinkle with salt and pepper to taste. Bake in preheated oven until fish is cooked through, about 10 to 12 minutes. Serve fish topped with sauce.

Tip: It is best to use fresh fish the same day or the following day after you purchase them. Store fish fillets in the refrigerator until ready to use.

Oven-Roasted Fish Fillets

Simplicity is the essence of this tasty dish. Salmon or halibut fillets are topped with sun-dried tomato pesto and fresh bread crumbs, then baked. If desired, fresh chopped herbs can be added to the crumb topping. The result is moist and flavorful fish. Serve with rice and a medley of fresh vegetables for a great weekday meal.

SERVES 4

- PREHEAT OVEN TO 400°F (200°C)
- 15-BY 10-INCH (1 L) BAKING SHEET, LINED WITH PARCHMENT PAPER

4	salmon or halibut fillets, each about 7 oz (200 g)	4
	Salt and freshly ground black pepper	
6 tbsp	Classico di Sardegna Sun-Dried Tomato Pesto	90 mL
1 cup	fresh bread crumbs (see Tip, below)	250 mL

1. Place fish fillets on prepared baking sheet. Sprinkle a little salt and pepper over each one. Spread 1¹/₂ tbsp (22 mL) pesto over each fillet. Top evenly with bread crumbs and gently press down.

2. Bake in preheated oven until fish is cooked through, about 12 to 15 minutes.

Tip: Fresh bread crumbs take no time to make. Freeze 2 slices white sandwich bread with crusts removed. Cut frozen bread into cubes. Place in food processor and process until fine crumbs form. For a nice flavor change, add 1 tbsp (15 mL) of your favorite chopped herb before processing. Makes about 1 cup (250 mL).

Halibut with Fennel and Tomato

If you haven't cooked with fennel, now is the time to add this aromatic vegetable to your repertoire. This simple bake, which returns fennel to its Mediterranean roots by pairing it with a roasted tomato and garlic sauce, is deliciously tempting.

SERVES 6

- PREHEAT OVEN TO 400°F (200°C)
- 13-BY 9-INCH (3 L) BAKING DISH

1	fennel, trimmed and thinly sliced (see Tip, below)	1
1	onion, sliced	1
2 tbsp	olive oil	25 mL
	Salt and freshly ground black pepper	
1	jar (26 oz/700 mL) Classico di Siena Fire-Roasted Tomato & Garlic Pasta Sauce	1
6	halibut fillets, each about 6 oz (175 g)	6

Variation
Replace halibut with sea bass, monkfish or cod.

1. Toss fennel and onion with olive oil. Season with salt and pepper to taste. Spread fennel-onion mixture in baking dish. Bake in preheated oven until just tender, about 25 minutes. Remove from oven.

2. Spoon half the sauce over fennel-onion mixture. Top with halibut fillets, then cover with remaining sauce. Return to oven and bake until fish is cooked through, about 12 to 14 minutes.

Tip: When buying fennel, look for firm, well-shaped white bulbs with green stalks and small leafy fronds. To trim the fennel, cut off the stalks where they join the bulb, then slice as required.

Crab-Stuffed Sole

Here's a dish that is remarkably uncomplicated, yet impressive enough for guests. Serve with fluffy white rice and asparagus spears for an elegant meal.

SERVES 4

Variation
Replace the sole with salmon.

- PREHEAT OVEN TO 350°F (180°C)
- 6-CUP (1.5 L) BAKING DISH

1⅓ cups	Classico di Firenze Florentine Spinach & Cheese Pasta Sauce	325 mL
½ cup	crumbled feta cheese	125 mL
4 oz	cooked crab meat, flaked	125 g
2 oz	cooked salad shrimp, chopped	60 g
3 tbsp	Classico di Genova Basil Pesto	45 mL
4	sole fillets, each about 5 to 6 oz (150 to 175 g)	4
	Chopped fresh parsley or basil, optional	

1. Spread pasta sauce in baking dish.

2. In a bowl, combine feta, crab, shrimp and pesto.

3. Spread about 4 tbsp (60 mL) crab mixture onto each fillet. Roll up and place seam-side down on sauce in baking dish. Cover and bake in preheated oven until the fish is cooked through, about 18 to 20 minutes. Serve topped with sauce and basil, if using.

Tip: To check if the fish is done, it should flake easily when tested with a fork.

Mediterranean Fish Stew

This is a rich-flavored fish stew that is simple to prepare and can easily be varied by the fish available at the market. For a true Italian touch, ladle the stew over toasted or grilled slices of rustic bread and expect requests for seconds.

SERVES 4 TO 6

2 tbsp	olive oil	25 mL
3	cloves garlic, minced	3
2	stalks celery, thinly sliced	2
1	onion, diced	1
2	sprigs fresh thyme	2
1 cup	water	250 mL
1	jar (26 oz/700 mL) Classico di Napoli Tomato & Basil Pasta Sauce	1
	Salt and freshly ground black pepper	
7 oz	halibut, cut into 1½-inch (4 cm) cubes	200 g
7 oz	cod, cut into 1½-inch (4 cm) cubes	200 g
7 oz	monkfish, cut into 1½-inch (4 cm) cubes	200 g

Variation
Try grouper or snapper for a nice change.

1. In a Dutch oven or large saucepan, heat oil over medium heat. Add garlic, celery and onion. Cook until vegetables are tender, about 7 to 8 minutes.

2. Add thyme, water and pasta sauce. Bring to a boil. Reduce heat to medium-low and simmer, covered, for 10 minutes. Season with salt and pepper to taste.

3. Add halibut, cod and monkfish. Simmer, covered, until fish is just cooked through, about 8 minutes. Remove thyme sprigs and serve.

Tip: Make ahead: This dish can be prepared up to Step 2 and refrigerated overnight. When you are ready to serve, simply reheat and add fish.

Seared Sea Scallops and Shrimp with Pesto and Couscous

If you like seafood, you'll love this delicious sauté. The couscous completes the Mediterranean theme and is ready in minutes.

Couscous

1½ cups	chicken stock or water	375 mL
1 tbsp	butter	15 mL
Pinch	salt	Pinch
1 cup	couscous	250 mL

Seafood

2 tbsp	butter	25 mL
8	large shrimp, peeled and deveined	8
12	large sea scallops	12
3 tbsp	lemon juice (or to taste)	45 mL
3 tbsp	vegetable or chicken stock (or to taste)	45 mL
3 tbsp	Classico di Genova Basil Pesto (or to taste)	45 mL

Variation
Add ½ cup (125 mL) sliced snow peas to cooking shrimp and scallops.

1. Couscous: In a medium saucepan, bring stock, butter and salt to a boil. Stir in couscous. Cover and remove from heat. Let stand for 5 to 6 minutes. Fluff with a fork.

2. Seafood: In a skillet, melt butter over medium-high heat. Add shrimp and cook until pink, about 2 to 3 minutes. Add scallops and cook until scallops and shrimp are cooked through, about 2 to 3 minutes more. Stir in lemon juice, stock and pesto. Cook until just heated through, about 1 to 2 minutes. Serve shrimp and scallops over bed of couscous.

Baked Red Snapper with Artichokes and Pesto

Here is very scrumptious fish dish that can be put together in minutes and then popped in the oven to bake.

- PREHEAT OVEN TO 400°F (200°C)
- 15-BY 10-INCH (1 L) BAKING SHEET

1 tbsp	olive oil	15 mL
1	onion, finely chopped	1
4 oz	white button mushrooms, sliced	125 g
1	can (14 oz/398 mL) artichoke hearts, drained and cut into quarters	1
12	cherry tomatoes, cut in half	12
¼ cup	dry white wine or chicken stock	50 mL
3 tbsp	Classico di Genova Basil Pesto	45 mL
6	red snapper fillets, each about 5 oz (150 g)	6
	Salt and freshly ground black pepper	

Variation

Substitute striped bass, pickerel or halibut for the red snapper.

1. In a skillet, heat oil over medium heat. Add onion and mushrooms. Cook until tender, about 7 to 8 minutes. Stir in artichoke hearts, tomatoes and wine. Cook until most of the wine has evaporated. Remove from heat and stir in pesto. Cool slightly.

2. Cut six pieces of parchment paper into 15-inch (37.5 cm) squares. Place one red snapper fillet on each paper. Lightly season with salt and pepper. Spoon artichoke mixture evenly over each piece.

3. Fold each paper to form a sealed packet. Place each packet on baking sheet and bake in preheated oven until the fish is cooked through, about 16 to 18 minutes.

Tip: Prepare this dish using your outdoor barbecue by making the packets out of heavy-duty foil, then place them over medium-high heat and cook until the fish flakes easily, about 15 to 18 minutes.

Seafood Trio Sauté

This appetizing medley of fish and seafood is nestled in a rich cream sauce. It looks beautiful served over a bed of cooked fettuccine or your favorite pasta.

SERVES 4

2 tbsp	butter	25 mL
1	shallot, finely chopped	1
½	yellow bell pepper, cut into strips	½
½	yellow zucchini, cut into strips	½
12 oz	salmon fillet, skin removed and cut into 1½-inch (4 cm) cubes, about 8 pieces	375 g
12	large shrimp, peeled and deveined	12
12	large scallops	12
⅓ cup	dry white wine	75 mL
1	jar (16 oz/ 435 mL) Classico Alfredo di Capri Sun-Dried Tomato Pasta Sauce	1
1 cup	frozen green peas, thawed	250 mL
8	cooked asparagus spears, sliced on the diagonal (see Tip, page 53)	8
	Chopped parsley or chives, optional	

1. In a large skillet, melt butter over medium heat. Add shallot, pepper and zucchini. Cook until tender, about 6 to 8 minutes.

2. Add salmon and shrimp and more butter, if required. Cook until shrimp are pink, about 2 to 3 minutes. Add scallops and wine. Cover and steam for 1 to 2 minutes. Stir in pasta sauce, peas and asparagus. Simmer (do not boil) for 2 to 3 minutes. Serve topped with parsley or chives, if using.

Tip: Yellow zucchini is sometimes referred to as crookneck or straightneck squash. If it is not available, use green zucchini instead.

Shrimp with Tomato and Feta

This Adriatic-inspired dish pairs feta cheese with shrimp and tomatoes, a marriage made in heaven. Better still, it's an easy dish to pull together on hectic days. For an interesting presentation, serve this over orzo, a tiny pasta that looks like rice.

SERVES 4

- PREHEAT BROILER
- 6-CUP (1.5 L) BAKING DISH

2 tbsp	olive oil	25 mL
3 to 4	cloves garlic, minced	3 to 4
1	onion, diced	1
⅓ cup	dry white wine, optional	75 mL
1 lb	large shrimp, peeled and deveined	500 g
¼ cup	chopped fresh parsley	50 mL
1⅓ cups	Classico di Firenze Florentine Spinach & Cheese Pasta Sauce	325 mL
	Salt and freshly ground black pepper	
1 cup	crumbled feta cheese	250 mL

1. In a skillet, heat oil over medium heat. Add garlic and onion. Cook until softened, about 6 to 7 minutes. Increase the heat to medium-high. Stir in wine, if using, and cook until most of the wine has evaporated. Add shrimp and cook until pink, about 2 to 3 minutes per side. Stir in parsley and pasta sauce. Bring to a boil. Reduce heat to medium and simmer for 1 to 2 minutes. Season with salt and pepper to taste.

2. Spoon mixture into baking dish. Sprinkle feta over top. Place under broiler until cheese melts, about 1 to 2 minutes.

Shrimp Jambalaya

Jambalaya is one of those dishes that changes with every recipe. Shrimp, sausage and rice tend to be the basics, but creative cooks often add ingredients on a whim. There is always a hit of heat in this one-pot dish. If you are cooking for diehard heat seekers, pass the hot pepper sauce or sprinkle with finely chopped chili pepper just before serving.

SERVES 4 TO 6

2 tbsp	olive oil	25 mL
2	stalks celery, sliced	2
1	onion, chopped	1
1	green bell pepper, seeded and chopped	1
12 oz	ham or smoked sausage, such as chorizo or kielbasa, cubed	375 g
1 lb	medium shrimp, peeled and deveined	500 g
2	cloves garlic, minced	2
1½ tsp	dried thyme leaves	7 mL
½ tsp	cayenne pepper	2 mL
¼ tsp	salt	1 mL
¼ tsp	freshly ground black pepper	1 mL
1½ cups	long-grain rice	375 mL
2 cups	chicken stock or water	500 mL
1	jar (26 oz/700 mL) Classico di Siena Fire-Roasted Tomato & Garlic Pasta Sauce	1

1. In a large saucepan, heat oil over medium heat. Add celery, onion, green pepper and ham. Cook until vegetables are tender, about 8 to 10 minutes. Add shrimp, garlic, thyme, cayenne, salt and pepper. Cook until shrimp are pink, about 2 to 3 minutes per side. Add rice and cook, stirring, for 1 minute.

2. Stir in stock and pasta sauce. Bring to a boil. Reduce heat to medium-low. Cover and cook until rice is tender but mixture is still moist, about 20 to 25 minutes.

Tip: To get every bit of sauce, swirl some of the stock around inside the jar before adding to saucepan.

Baked Cod with Vegetables

Here's an intriguing recipe that does double duty: it's a great weekday meal or an impressive dish for guests. Flavorful cod is baked in parchment paper with vegetables and sun-dried tomato pesto, producing a moist and savory result. Serve with rice and a green vegetable for a great meal.

SERVES 4

• PREHEAT OVEN TO 400°F (200°C)
• 15-BY 10-INCH (1 L) BAKING SHEET

1	leek, white and light green part only, washed (see Tip, page 28)	1
1	carrot, peeled	1
2 tbsp	butter	25 mL
¼ cup	chicken or vegetable stock	50 mL
3 tbsp	Classico di Sardegna Sun-Dried Tomato Pesto	45 mL
4	cod fillets, each about 6 oz (175 g)	4
	Salt and freshly ground black pepper	

1. Cut leek and carrot into matchstick strips.

2. In a skillet, melt butter over medium heat. Add leek and carrot. Cook until tender, about 7 to 8 minutes. Stir in stock and simmer for 1 minute. Stir in pesto. Cool slightly.

3. Cut four pieces of parchment paper into 15-inch (37.5 cm) squares. Place one cod fillet on each paper. Lightly season with salt and pepper. Spoon leek mixture evenly over each piece.

4. Fold each paper to form a sealed packet. Place each packet on baking sheet and bake in preheated oven until the fish is cooked through, about 20 minutes.

Tip: If you don't have parchment paper on hand, foil can be used to make the packets.

Variation
Substitute pickerel, salmon, swordfish or halibut for the cod.

Vegetarian, Vegetables and Side Dishes

Tomato-Roasted Potatoes

Tomato-Roasted Potatoes

If you're tired of the same old potatoes, here's a recipe that will invigorate your taste buds. Combining peeled potatoes with olive oil and sun-dried tomato sauce before baking makes for a hearty, rustic dish.

SERVES 6

- PREHEAT OVEN TO 425°F (220°C)
- 13-BY 9-INCH (3 L) BAKING DISH

2 lbs	medium Yukon Gold potatoes, about 6	1 kg
2 tbsp	vegetable oil	25 mL
¼ tsp	salt	1 mL
¼ tsp	freshly ground black pepper	1 mL
1⅓ cups	Classico di Capri Sun-Dried Tomato Pasta Sauce	325 mL
1¾ cups	water	425 mL

1. Peel potatoes and cut lengthwise into 6 wedges. Toss potatoes with oil, salt and pepper. Arrange in baking dish.

2. Stir together pasta sauce and water. Pour over potato wedges. Roast in preheated oven until sauce is thickened and potatoes are tender, about 60 to 70 minutes.

Variation

As soon as potatoes come out of the oven, sprinkle with ¾ cup (175 mL) old Cheddar, Monterey Jack or Asiago cheese. Let stand until melted.

Layered Eggplant Casserole

Here is an easy dish that is delicious and the perfect solution for time-pressed days. For a delectable meal, serve this alongside sliced tomatoes drizzled with a balsamic vinaigrette.

SERVES 6 TO 8

- PREHEAT OVEN TO 350°F (180°C)
- 8-CUP (2 L) BAKING DISH OR CASSEROLE

	Salt	
2	large eggplants, sliced into ½-inch (1 cm) rounds	2
	All purpose flour	
1½ cups	olive oil (approx.)	375 mL
1	jar (26 oz/700 mL) Classico di Parma Four Cheese Pasta Sauce	1
1½ cups	shredded mozzarella cheese	375 mL
⅓ cup	freshly grated Parmesan cheese	75 mL
	Additional grated Parmesan cheese, optional	

1. Lightly salt eggplant rounds and let stand 30 minutes. Wipe off salt and pat dry. Lightly toss in flour, then remove and set aside.

2. In a large skillet, heat 6 tbsp (90 mL) oil over medium-high heat. Fry eggplant rounds, 2 or 3 at a time, cooking until both sides are golden, adding more oil when required. Place cooked eggplant on paper towel-lined trays to absorb excess oil.

3. Spread a thin layer of sauce in baking dish. Top with one-third of eggplant, one-third of sauce, half of mozzarella cheese and one-third of Parmesan cheese. Repeat layers ending with eggplant. Top with remaining sauce and Parmesan cheese.

4. Bake, uncovered, in preheated oven for 25 to 30 minutes. Let stand for 15 minutes before serving. Top with additional cheese before serving, if desired.

Variation

Substitute grated Romano cheese for Parmesan cheese.

Roasted Vegetable Frittata with Goat Cheese

Frittata is an Italian omelet that incorporates the flavoring ingredients into the eggs. Because it isn't folded, it is easier to make than a French-style omelet. As eggs combine well with so many ingredients, frittatas are a versatile dish. They are also a quick and easy choice for brunch or even supper. This one is special enough for company.

SERVES 6

- PREHEAT BROILER
- 9-INCH (23 CM) OVENPROOF SKILLET

8	eggs	8
¼ cup	milk	50 mL
3 tbsp	Classico di Genova Basil Pesto	45 mL
½ tsp	salt	2 mL
1 tsp	vegetable oil	5 mL
2 cups	assorted roasted vegetables (see Tip, below)	500 mL
3 oz	goat cheese, crumbled	90 g

1. Whisk together eggs, milk, pesto and salt.

2. In a skillet over medium-high heat, heat oil. Add roasted vegetables and cook until sizzling. Pour in egg mixture. Reduce heat to medium. Cook until bottom and sides are set but top is still runny, about 10 to 12 minutes.

3. Sprinkle cheese over top. Place in oven and broil until top is golden and set, about 3 to 5 minutes.

Tip: Roasted vegetables are easy and versatile. Make a batch for dinner and include extra to have on hand for frittatas, omelets or to add to a pasta sauce. Cut assorted vegetables, such as eggplant, zucchini, bell peppers, mushrooms and sweet potatoes, into 1-inch (2.5 cm) pieces. Toss with oil. Sprinkle with salt and pepper. Roast in 425°F (220°C) oven, stirring once, until tender and golden brown, about 25 minutes.

Vegetarian Chili

Don't let the length of ingredients in this recipe alarm you. This dish is simple to make and has an abundance of healthy foods. If you prefer a spicier version, add a finely chopped jalapeño pepper along with the potatoes.

SERVES 6 TO 8

3 tbsp	olive oil	45 mL
2	onions, chopped	2
4 to 5	garlic cloves, chopped	4 to 5
2	new white potatoes, peeled and cubed	2
2	sweet potatoes, peeled and cubed	2
2	carrots, peeled and cubed	2
2	jars (each 26 oz/ 700 mL) Classico di Siena Fire-Roasted Tomato & Garlic Pasta Sauce	2
1	can (19 oz/540 mL) red kidney beans, drained and rinsed	1
1	can (19 oz/540 mL) chickpeas, drained and rinsed	1
2 tsp	chili powder	10 mL
1 tsp	paprika	5 mL
½ tsp	cayenne pepper	2 mL
	Salt and freshly ground black pepper	
	Sour cream, optional	

Variation
Adjust the spice level to suit your liking.

1. In a large saucepan, heat oil over medium heat. Add onions and garlic. Cook for 4 to 5 minutes. Add potatoes, sweet potatoes and carrots. Cook for 7 to 8 minutes. Stir in pasta sauce, beans, chickpeas, chili powder, paprika and cayenne. Season with salt and pepper to taste. Bring to a boil. Reduce heat, cover and simmer, stirring occasionally, for 40 minutes or until vegetables are tender. Serve topped with sour cream, if using.

Tip: This recipe freezes very well for up to 2 months. Pack in containers that can be popped in the microwave. Reheat thawed container on medium-high power for 2 to 3 minutes or until warmed through, stirring after 1 minute.

Genoa Pizza

Here's a pizza that is ideal for quick dinners. Light tasting and colorful, with the addition of a tossed salad, it makes a great family meal.

SERVES 4 TO 6

- PREHEAT OVEN TO 425°C (220°C)
- BAKING SHEET OR PIZZA PAN

½ cup	Classico di Genova Basil Pesto	125 mL
1	ready-made 12-inch (30 cm) pizza crust or dough	1
¼ cup	freshly grated Parmesan cheese	50 mL
1	tomato, thinly sliced	1
½ cup	ricotta cheese	125 mL
¼ cup	crumbled feta cheese	50 mL
2 tbsp	chopped fresh basil	25 mL

1. Spread pesto over crust, leaving a ½-inch (1 cm) border. Sprinkle Parmesan cheese over pesto layer. Arrange tomato slices, ricotta and feta cheese over top. Sprinkle with basil.

2. Place on baking sheet or pizza pan and bake in preheated oven until cheese has melted, about 12 to 15 minutes.

Variation
Try topping with a handful of chopped fresh or cooked spinach leaves.

Grilled Vegetable Pizza

Homemade pizza is a great meal planner for today's busy families. This version, which uses grilled vegetables, is both tasty and nutritious. Serve with soup to complete the meal.

SERVES 4 TO 6

- PREHEAT OVEN TO 425°F (220°C)
- BAKING SHEET OR PIZZA PAN

1	ready-made 12-inch (30 cm) pizza crust or dough	1
1 cup	Classico di Genoa Tomato & Pesto Pasta Sauce	250 mL
1½ cups	grated mozzarella cheese	375 mL
1 cup	chopped assorted grilled vegetables, such as zucchini, asparagus, bell peppers and mushrooms (see Tip, page 44)	250 mL
2 oz	goat cheese, crumbled	60 g
1 tbsp	assorted chopped fresh herbs, such as parsley, basil, oregano and thyme	15 mL

1. Top pizza crust with sauce and mozzarella cheese. Spread vegetables evenly over cheese layer. Sprinkle top with goat cheese and herbs.

2. Place on baking sheet or pizza pan and bake in preheated oven for 15 minutes or until cheese has melted. Let stand at least 5 minutes before cutting.

Tip: Prepare the pizza in advance and store covered in the refrigerator until ready to bake.

Variation

Substitute the grilled vegetables for 1 cup (250 mL) steamed broccoli florets and a tablespoon (15 mL) diced roasted red bell pepper.

Leek, Gruyère and Sun-Dried Tomato Pesto Tart

Here's a wonderful brunch dish that invites improvisation. You'll want to re-invent it again and again trying your own additions or some of the variations suggested below. Serve with a crisp green salad and cold white wine and wait for the compliments to flow.

SERVES 4

- PREHEAT OVEN TO 400°F (200°C)
- PLACE RACK ON BOTTOM RUNG

1	frozen 9-inch (23 cm) deep-dish pie shell	1
1	leek, white and light green parts only	1
1 tbsp	vegetable oil	15 mL
3 tbsp	Classico di Sardegna Sun-Dried Tomato Pesto	45 mL
¾ cup	shredded Gruyère cheese	175 mL
4	eggs	4
1¼ cups	milk	300 mL
¼ tsp	freshly ground black pepper	1 mL

1. Thaw pie shell, if necessary, according to package instructions. Pierce bottom all over with fork. Line with foil and fill with pie weights or dried beans. Bake on baking sheet on bottom rack of preheated oven until rim is golden brown, about 12 to 15 minutes. Remove foil and weights. Let cool. Reduce oven temperature to 375°F (190°C).

2. Meanwhile, halve leek lengthwise. Rinse under running water and drain well. Slice thinly. In a small skillet, heat oil over medium heat. Cook leek until tender, about 3 to 5 minutes.

3. Spread pesto over bottom of cooled pie shell. Sprinkle with half the Gruyère, then leeks. Whisk together eggs, milk and pepper. Pour over cheese and leeks. Sprinkle with remaining cheese. Place on a baking sheet. Bake on bottom rack of oven until toothpick inserted in center comes out clean, about 35 to 40 minutes.

Variations

Add 4 slices of bacon, cooked and crumbled.

Add 1 cooked cubed potato.

Instead of leeks, use 6 spears cooked asparagus, cut into 1-inch (2.5 cm) pieces.

Substitute Cheddar or Jarlsberg cheese for the Gruyère.

Baked Stuffed Zucchini

Zucchini leaves its mild reputation behind with this cheese and mushroom stuffing and a tangy tomato sauce. Double this recipe for a great potluck dish. To increase eye appeal, add a salad of multicolored sweet peppers, roasted and tossed in olive oil.

SERVES 2
OR 4 AS A
SIDE DISH

• PREHEAT OVEN TO 425°F (220°C)
• 11-BY 7-INCH (2 L) BAKING DISH

2	zucchini	2
1 tbsp	butter	15 mL
2/3 cup	chopped mushrooms	150 mL
1/3 cup	chopped onion, about 1/2 a medium onion	75 mL
1	clove garlic, minced	1
1/4 tsp	salt	1 mL
1 1/3 cups	Classico di Toscana Portobello Mushroom Pasta Sauce	325 mL
2/3 cup	fresh bread crumbs	150 mL
2/3 cup	grated old Cheddar cheese	150 mL

1. Cut zucchini in half lengthwise. Trim bottom of each slightly to level. With small spoon, scoop flesh from each half and dice. Set aside.

2. In a skillet, melt butter over medium-high heat. Add diced zucchini, mushrooms, onion, garlic and salt. Cook until golden brown and softened, about 4 to 6 minutes. Stir in 3 tbsp (45 mL) pasta sauce. Remove from heat. Stir in bread crumbs, then Cheddar.

3. Pour remaining pasta sauce into baking dish. Place zucchini halves in dish. Divide stuffing between zucchini halves, packing tightly. Cover and bake in preheated oven for 20 minutes. Uncover and cook until zucchini is tender, about 10 to 15 minutes more. Serve with a chickpea salad and sliced red pepper.

Roasted Vegetable Spread with Olives and Pesto

This delicious antipasto is the perfect dish to have on hand for unexpected guests. Not only is it versatile, but roasting makes the vegetables intensely flavorful. Spoon it onto crackers, a toasted baguette or focaccia. It's also great swirled into a cream soup, on top of a cheese melt or added to a pasta salad. Use your imagination and enjoy.

MAKES 2½ CUPS (625 ML)

- PREHEAT OVEN TO 450°F (230°C)
- BAKING SHEET, GREASED

2	bell peppers (any color)	2
1	zucchini	1
1	onion	1
½	eggplant	½
¼ cup	olive oil	50 mL
¼ cup	Classico di Sardegna Sun-Dried Tomato Pesto	50 mL
⅓ cup	chopped black olives	75 mL

1. Core and seed peppers. Trim ends from zucchini. Peel onion and eggplant. Cut all vegetables into ½-inch (1 cm) pieces. Toss with olive oil. Spread on prepared baking sheet.

2. Roast in preheated oven, stirring occasionally, until browned and soft, about 25 to 35 minutes.

3. While still warm, toss vegetables with pesto and olives. Let cool. Mixture can be refrigerated in an airtight container for up to 1 week.

Tip: Stir vegetables more frequently during the last 15 minutes of baking, when they are already browning.

Tip: To make a double batch, spread on 2 baking sheets. Roast, switching trays every 10 minutes, for 40 to 50 minutes.

Creamy Mushroom Risotto

Risotto, a creamy blend of seasoned rice and other ingredients that is cooked slowly and most often served as a main course, is a wonderfully comforting dish. This version is particularly rich and decadent.

SERVES 6

2 tbsp	olive oil	25 mL
2 to 3	cloves garlic, minced	2 to 3
1 lb	assorted mushrooms, such as shiitake, cremini or button mushrooms, sliced	500 g
1½ cups	Arborio rice (see Tip, below)	375 mL
5 cups	hot vegetable stock (approx.)	1.25 mL
1⅓ cups	Classico di Parma Four Cheese Pasta Sauce	325 mL
1 cup	frozen green peas, thawed and blanched	500 mL
3 tbsp	freshly grated Parmesan cheese	45 mL
	Salt and freshly ground black pepper	
¼ cup	assorted chopped fresh herbs, such as parsley, basil and thyme	50 mL
	Additional freshly grated Parmesan cheese, optional	

Variation
Replace the peas and stir in 1 cup (250 mL) chopped roasted vegetables along with the sauce.

1. In a large saucepan, heat oil over medium-high heat. Add garlic and mushrooms. Cook until tender, about 7 to 8 minutes. Add rice and cook, stirring, for 2 to 3 minutes. Reduce heat to medium-low. Add ½ cup (125 mL) stock and cook, stirring, until stock is absorbed. Continue to add ½ cup (125 mL) stock at a time, stirring until it is absorbed. Repeat process until all the stock is used and the rice is just tender and creamy, adding more stock, if required.

2. Stir in pasta sauce and peas. Cook and stir until heated through, about 2 to 3 minutes. Remove from the heat. Stir in Parmesan cheese. Season with salt and pepper to taste.

3. Serve risotto topped with herbs and additional Parmesan, if using.

Tip: It is important to use short-grain rice such as Arborio to achieve the creamy texture of this dish. If you can't find Arborio rice, then look for carnaroli or vialone nano varieties of short-grain rice.

Entertaining

~

Roasted Cornish Hens with Pesto

Roasted Cornish Hens with Pesto

The combination of flavors in this sophisticated dish will please all your guests. Serve this dish with a simple rice pilaf topped with toasted pine nuts and a side of steamed carrots tossed with butter. Add fresh fruit for dessert.

SERVES 4

- PREHEAT OVEN TO 400°F (200°C)
- ROASTING RACK AND PAN

2	Cornish hens, each about 1½ lbs (750 g)	2
	Salt and freshly ground black pepper	
2	sprigs fresh thyme or tarragon	2
2	whole cloves garlic, peeled	2
½	lemon, cut into 2 wedges	½
5 tbsp	Classico di Sardegna Sun-Dried Tomato Pesto (approx.)	75 mL
4 to 6	slices prosciutto	4 to 6

Variation
Use thinly sliced pancetta in place of the prosciutto.

1. Place each hen on a flat surface and gently force your fingers between the skin and breast meat to loosen the skin and create a pocket. Lightly season hens with salt and pepper.

2. Place one sprig of thyme, garlic clove and lemon wedge in the cavity of each hen. Tie the legs with string to secure.

3. Spread enough pesto in pocket of each hen and all over skin to coat, about 2 to 3 tbsp (25 to 45 mL). Wrap 2 to 3 pieces prosciutto around each of the Cornish hens, tucking under to secure.

4. Place hens on rack in shallow roasting pan and bake in preheated oven until the meat is cooked through and no longer pink inside, about 30 to 35 minutes. Let stand for 5 minutes before cutting in half and serving.

Tip: This recipe works great with a small roasting chicken as well. Increase the prosciutto by 2 to 3 slices. Increase roasting time to 55 minutes or until no longer pink inside. Make sure to cover prosciutto with foil if browning too much.

Sausage and Pesto-Stuffed Turkey Breast

The beauty of this recipe is that once assembled, it cooks happily in the oven, leaving you free to do other things. Your guests will find this tasty dish hard to resist and you can take great satisfaction in knowing it took no time to prepare.

SERVES 6

• PREHEAT OVEN TO 325°F (160°C)

4 oz	mild Italian sausage	125 g
1/3 cup	chopped celery, about 1/2 a stalk	75 mL
1/3 cup	chopped red bell pepper, about 1/2 a pepper	75 mL
3/4 cup	fresh bread crumbs	175 mL
3 tbsp	Classico di Genova Basil Pesto	45 mL
1	boneless single turkey breast, skin on, about 2 lbs (1 kg)	1
	Salt and freshly ground black pepper	

1. Remove sausage from casing and break into small pieces. In a skillet over medium heat, cook sausage, celery and red pepper until sausage is no longer pink and vegetables are tender, about 5 to 7 minutes. Remove from heat and cool. Stir in bread crumbs and pesto.

2. Place turkey breast skin-side down on cutting board. With a sharp knife held horizontally, slice into long side of breast almost but not all the way through to the other side. Open up like a book. Spoon stuffing onto one side of breast, leaving a 1-inch (2.5 cm) border. Fold other side over to enclose stuffing. Secure edges with toothpicks. Place on rack in roasting pan. Sprinkle with salt and pepper to taste.

3. Roast in preheated oven until juices run clear when pierced, about 1¼ to 1½ hours. Tent with foil and let stand for 10 minutes before slicing.

Tip: Ask your butcher to butterfly the turkey breast for you.

Pesto-Crusted Rack of Lamb with Feta

Here's a sensational recipe for those times when you need to pull out all the stops and impress your guests. A rack of lamb is roasted in a crust of basil pesto and feta cheese. Add roasted potatoes, mixed beans and a full-bodied red wine for an extraordinary meal.

SERVES 2 TO 3

- PREHEAT OVEN TO 400°F (200°C)
- ROASTING RACK AND PAN

½ cup	crumbled feta cheese	125 mL
⅓ cup	Classico di Genova Basil Pesto	75 mL
1	rack of lamb, trimmed, about 1½ lbs (750 g)	1
	Salt and freshly ground black pepper	
1 cup	fresh parsley bread crumbs (see Tip, below)	250 mL

1. Combine feta cheese with pesto.

2. Season lamb with salt and pepper. Place on rack in shallow roasting pan. Bake in preheated oven for 30 minutes.

3. Remove lamb from oven. Spread feta-pesto mixture on top of lamb and gently press in bread crumbs to form a crust. Return lamb to oven and bake until meat thermometer reads 150°F (70°C) for medium-rare, about 12 to 15 minutes more, or continue cooking until the lamb is done to your liking. (If the crust is browning too quickly, cover with foil.) Let stand for 5 minutes before slicing.

Tip: This recipe can be doubled when two racks of lamb are required.

Tip: Parsley Bread Crumbs: To prepare fresh parsley bread crumbs, freeze 2 slices white sandwich bread with crusts removed. (Freezing results in very fine textured bread crumbs.) Cut frozen bread into cubes. Place in food processor along with 1 tbsp (15 mL) chopped fresh parsley and process until fine crumbs form. Makes about 1 cup (250 mL).

Veal Cutlets with Shiitake Mushrooms and Pesto Cream

Fresh shiitake mushrooms, which used to be an exotic treat, are now readily available in many supermarket produce departments. Serve this exquisite dish with roasted mini potatoes and steamed broccoli for a great easy-to-prepare meal.

SERVES 4

2 tbsp	all-purpose flour	25 mL
¼ tsp	salt	1 mL
1 lb	veal cutlets, about ¼-inch (0.5 cm) thick	500 g
3 tbsp	vegetable oil, divided	45 mL
3 cups	stemmed and sliced shiitake mushrooms, about 8 oz (250 g) whole (see Tip, right)	750 mL
1 cup	whipping (35%) cream	250 mL
½	red bell pepper, thinly sliced	½
2 tbsp	Classico di Sardegna Sun-Dried Tomato Pesto	25 mL

Variation
Replace veal with turkey cutlets and Classico di Sardegna Sun-Dried Tomato Pesto with Classico di Genova Basil Pesto.

1. Combine flour and salt on a plate. Dredge cutlets in flour, shaking off and discarding excess.

2. In a skillet, heat 1½ tbsp (22 mL) oil over medium-high heat. Cook cutlets, in batches, until golden brown, about 2 minutes per side. Transfer to plate and keep warm.

3. Add remaining oil and mushrooms to pan. Cook until softened, about 3 to 5 minutes. Add cream and red pepper and bring to a boil. Boil gently until thick enough to coat the back of a spoon, about 3 to 5 minutes. Stir in pesto.

4. Return veal and any juices to pan for 1 minute, turning to coat and warm through. Serve at once.

....

Tip: Mushroom options: If you can't find fresh shiitake mushrooms, use button. For an exotic mushroom flavor, rehydrate 1 package ($^1/_2$ oz/14 g) dried mushrooms in 1 cup (250 mL) boiling water. Chop rehydrated mushrooms and add to pan with button mushrooms.

Tip: Thin slices of meat and poultry, such as turkey, can also be referred to as scaloppini and used in this recipe.

Other Great Recipes Featuring
Classico di Sardegna
Sun-Dried Tomato Pesto

Appetizers
Artichoke and Sun-Dried Tomato Salad (*page 41*)
Sun-Dried Tomato, Mushroom and Goat Cheese Toasts (*page 16*)
Tomato Chili Hummus (*page 24*)

Fish
Oven-Roasted Fish Fillets (*page 136*)

Meat
Sun-Dried Tomato Pesto and Cheese-Stuffed Pork Chops (*page 97*)

Salads
Chickpea Salad with Grilled Shrimp (*page 38*)
Three-Bean and Corn Salad (*page 37*)

For a complete list of recipes using this sauce,
see Index by Sauce (*page 185*).

Golden Cherry Tomato and Pesto Tart

Brunch is a perfect opportunity for relaxed, easy entertaining — this savory tart fits the bill. The tomatoes and pesto are a great flavor combination, and the tart can be made in advance and reheated just before serving.

SERVES 4

- PREHEAT OVEN TO 400°F (200°C)
- PLACE RACK ON BOTTOM RUNG

1	frozen 9-inch (23 cm) pie shell	1
8 oz	asparagus	250 g
2 oz	goat cheese, crumbled	60 g
½ cup	cubed ham, optional	125 mL
3	eggs	3
⅓ cup	whipping (35%) cream	75 mL
¼ cup	Classico di Genova Basil Pesto	50 mL
1 cup	yellow and red cherry tomatoes, halved	250 mL
½ tsp	freshly ground black pepper	2 mL

1. Thaw pie shell, if necessary, according to package instructions. Pierce bottom all over with fork. Line with foil and fill with pie weights or dried beans. Place on a baking sheet and bake on bottom rack of preheated oven until rim is golden brown, about 12 to 15 minutes. Remove foil and weights. Let cool. Reduce oven temperature to 375°F (190°C).

2. Trim woody ends from asparagus. Cut into 2-inch (5 cm) pieces. In pan of salted boiling water, cook asparagus for 3 to 4 minutes.

3. Sprinkle goat cheese in pie shell. Add asparagus, then ham, if using. Whisk together eggs, cream and pesto. Pour into pie shell. Place cherry tomatoes, cut-side up, on top. Sprinkle with pepper. Place on baking sheet. Bake on bottom rack of oven until toothpick inserted in center comes out clean, about 35 to 40 minutes.

Tip: Yellow cherry tomatoes are most often found in season at specialty green grocers. Regular cherry tomatoes or other tiny tomato varieties, such as grape or teardrop, can be substituted.

Spicy Italian Seafood Stew

Here's a great seafood stew that is a meal in itself. All you need to add is crusty Italian bread to soak up the sauce.

2 tbsp	olive oil	25 mL
4	cloves garlic, chopped	4
2	carrots, peeled and sliced into ¼-inch (0.5 cm) rounds	2
1	onion, finely diced	1
1 cup	sliced mushrooms	250 mL
1 cup	dry white wine	250 mL
1	jar (26 oz/700 mL) Classico di Roma Arrabbiata Spicy Red Pepper Pasta Sauce	1
1	can (14 oz/398 mL) artichoke hearts, drained and cut into quarters	1
12	sea scallops	12
12	large shrimp, peeled and deveined	12
	Salt	

Variation

Add cubed cod or sea bass for a subtle change.

1. In Dutch oven or large saucepan, heat oil over medium heat. Add garlic, carrots and onion. Cook until softened, about 8 to 10 minutes. Add mushrooms and cook 5 minutes more. Stir in wine, pasta sauce and artichoke hearts. Bring to a boil. Reduce heat to medium-low and simmer, stirring occasionally, for 10 minutes.

2. Stir in scallops and shrimp. Simmer, covered, until scallops are opaque and shrimp are pink and cooked through, about 3 minutes. Season with salt to taste.

Zucchini, Smoked Ham and Sun-Dried Tomato Risotto

The ultimate rice dish, this flavorful risotto works well as a first course or main meal. For an easy dinner party, serve marinated olives and a cheese plate to start, add a salad and finish with a fresh fruit tart.

SERVES 6

5 cups	chicken or vegetable stock (see Tip, below)	1.25 L
2 tbsp	olive oil	25 mL
½	onion, finely chopped	½
½	stalk celery, finely chopped	½
1	zucchini, diced	1
1½ cups	Arborio rice	375 mL
5 oz	smoked ham, diced	150 g
3 tbsp	Classico di Sardegna Sun-Dried Tomato Pesto (or to taste)	45 mL
	Salt and freshly ground black pepper	

Variation
Use grilled zucchini slices that have been cut into strips in place of the sautéed. Stir in with pesto and use to garnish dish.

1. In a saucepan, bring stock to a simmer on stovetop. Keep hot.

2. In a large saucepan, heat oil over medium heat. Add onion, celery and zucchini. Cook until vegetables are tender, about 7 to 8 minutes. Add rice and ham. Cook, stirring, for 2 to 3 minutes. Reduce heat to medium-low. Add ½ cup (125 mL) stock and cook, stirring, until stock is absorbed. Continue to add ½ cup (125 mL) stock at a time, stirring, until stock is absorbed. Repeat process until all the stock is used and rice is just tender and creamy.

3. Stir in pesto sauce. Season with salt and pepper to taste.

Tip: Hot stock is required to facilitate the breakdown of the starch in the rice. If cold stock is used it will be difficult to achieve the correct consistency of the dish, plus it will take a very long time to cook the rice.

Leek and Three-Cheese Stuffed Shells

Extend a warm welcome to your guests with this great comfort food dish. Made with a minimum of last-minute fuss, it takes the stress out of entertaining.

• PREHEAT OVEN TO 350°F (180°C)
• 13-BY 9-INCH (3.5 L) BAKING DISH

20	jumbo pasta shells	20
2 tbsp	olive oil	25 mL
1	leek, white and light green part only, washed and finely chopped (see Tip, page 28)	1
2 cups	ricotta cheese	500 mL
½ cup	grated Asiago cheese	125 mL
½ cup	shredded Fontina cheese	125 mL
	Salt and freshly ground black pepper	
1	egg, beaten	1
1	jar (26 oz/700 mL) Classico di Parma Four Cheese Pasta Sauce	1

Variation
Replace 1 cup (250 mL) ricotta with feta cheese and the Asiago with Romano cheese.

1. Cook jumbo shells according to package directions.

2. In a skillet, heat oil over medium heat. Add leek and cook until tender, about 6 to 7 minutes. Remove from heat and cool.

3. Mix together leek, ricotta, Asiago and Fontina cheeses. Season with salt and pepper to taste. Stir in egg until well combined.

4. Spread half of sauce in baking dish. Fill shells with about 3 tbsp (45 mL) leek-cheese mixture. Place in a single layer in prepared dish. Spoon remaining sauce over top. Cover and bake in preheated oven until filling is hot, about 30 to 35 minutes.

Tip: This recipe freezes well. Bake shells and cool. Freeze in microwave-safe containers or oven-to-freezer-safe baking dishes. Freeze for up to 2 months. Thaw in refrigerator. Reheat, covered, in 325°F (160°C) oven until heated through, about 25 minutes, or on medium power in microwave oven until heated through, about 5 to 6 minutes.

Seared Halibut with Mussels and Clams

Don't let a lack of time deter you from entertaining. Here's a tasty seafood dish that is brimming with flavor and texture and takes no time to prepare. For a quick and easy dinner, start with proscuitto-wrapped melon, add steamed new potatoes and blanched green beans to the main course and finish with fresh berries and cream.

SERVES 4

- PREHEAT OVEN TO 400°F (200°C)
- OVENPROOF SKILLET

4	halibut fillets (each about 5 oz/150 g), skin removed	4
	Salt and freshly ground black pepper	
1½ tbsp	olive oil, divided	22 mL
1½ tbsp	butter, divided	22 mL
2	shallots, finely chopped	2
½ cup	chicken or fish stock	125 mL
½ cup	dry white wine	125 mL
12	mussels, cleaned (see Tip, page 182)	12
8	littleneck clams	8
½	roasted red pepper, diced (see Tip, page 70)	½
1 tbsp	Classico di Genova Basil Pesto (or to taste)	15 mL

1. Season halibut with salt and pepper. Set aside.

2. In an ovenproof skillet, heat all but 1 tsp (5 mL) oil and butter over medium-high heat. Add halibut and cook for 1 to 2 minutes per side. Transfer skillet to preheated oven and bake until fish flakes easily and is cooked through, about 5 to 6 minutes. Remove and keep warm.

Variation
Substitute the halibut with monkfish or sea bass.

3. Meanwhile, in a Dutch oven or large saucepan, heat remaining oil and butter over medium-high heat. Add shallots and cook for 1 to 2 minutes. Add stock and wine. Bring to a boil. Add mussels and clams. Reduce heat to medium. Cover and simmer until mussels and clams open, about 4 to 6 minutes. If mussels open before clams, remove mussels and continue cooking until clams open. Remove from heat. Discard any shellfish that did not open. Stir in diced pepper and pesto. Serve shellfish topped with halibut and pesto broth.

Tip: Have the fishmonger remove the skin from the fillets.

Tip: Buy and prepare a few extra mussels and clams in case some don't open during cooking.

Other Great Recipes Featuring
Classico di Genova Basil Pesto

Appetizers
Brie and Onion Bake (*page 25*)
Eggplant and Cheese Rolls (*page 17*)

Chicken
Chicken and Asparagus Toss (*page 112*)
Chicken Meatballs (*page 120*)

Fish and Seafood
Baked Red Snapper with Artichokes and Pesto (*page 143*)
Crab-Stuffed Sole (*page 139*)

Vegetarian
Roasted Vegetable Frittata with Goat Cheese (*page 154*)

For a complete list of recipes using this sauce,
see Index by Sauce (*page 185*).

Steamed Mussels in a Spicy Tomato Broth

*This is one of the quickest and best ways to serve fresh mussels —
steamed in a flavorful broth of tomatoes, garlic and wine. Make
sure to have plenty of lightly toasted bread on hand and soup spoons
to enjoy every bit of the sauce.*

SERVES 4

1 tbsp	olive oil	15 mL
2	shallots, sliced	2
3	cloves garlic, minced	3
1 cup	dry white wine	250 mL
1	jar (26 oz/700 mL) Classico di Roma Arrabbiata Spicy Red Pepper Pasta Sauce	1
4 lbs	mussels, cleaned (see Tip, below)	2 kg
¼ cup	chopped fresh parsley or basil	50 mL
	Salt and freshly ground black pepper	

1. In a large saucepan, heat oil over medium heat. Add shallots and garlic. Cook for 3 to 4 minutes. Increase heat to medium-high. Add wine and pasta sauce. Bring to a boil. Add mussels. Reduce heat to medium. Cover and steam until the mussels open, about 5 to 7 minutes. Scoop mussels into serving bowls, discarding any that have not opened.

2. Stir parsley into sauce and season with salt and pepper to taste. Simmer for 1 to 2 minutes, and then ladle the sauce over mussels.

Tip: Clean mussels by brushing the shells under cold running water to loosen sand and grit, then cut or pull off the small tuft of fibers sticking out the side of the mussels known as the beard. It is best to clean mussels just before cooking.

National Library of Canada Cataloguing in Publication

Dallas, Antigone
      The Classico pasta sauce cookbook: start with Classico and create tempting home
cooked meals / by Antigone Dallas.

Includes index.
ISBN 0-7788-0057-1

1. Cookery. 2. Cookery (Pasta) I. Title.

TX819.A1D34 2002   641.5   C2002-901842-0

Index by Sauce

Index